Meher Baba's Man in Europe

a Memoir of Don Stevens

Michael Morice

Copyright © 2017 by Michael Morice

All rights reserved

ISBN 978-0-692-86253-7

Contact michaelmorice@gmail.com

Image of Don Stevens, Cagnes Sur Mer, May 1980
permission of Hasan Selisik

Image of Don Stevens and Eruch Jessawala in Mandali Hall
permission of David Lee

Image of Don Stevens and Michael Morice
permission of Sebastian Baker

Image of Don Stevens at Kailash temple
permission of Karl Moeller

Other images © Meher Nazar Publications

Book design by Karl Moeller

Font Hoefler Text

Meher Baba's Man in Europe

a Memoir of Don Stevens

Michael Morice

Meher Baba's Man in Europe
A Memoir of Don Stevens

Table of Contents

1	Meher Baba
7	Foreword by Craig san Roque
9	Preface by Rick Chapman
13	Introduction
17	London
81	Europe
89	Beads On A String
107	Don's Writing, Some Reflections
119	Forgiveness
130	Endnotes
147	Acknowledgements

Meher Baba at Qutub Minar, Delhi, India 1930s

MEHER BABA.

Nothing that follows would have been written, were it not for the presence of Meher Baba in the lives of all that are mentioned in my story. He is the lynchpin, the linking thread running through the narrative from beginning to end, and therefore a short introduction is in order for those who may not be familiar with Him.

He was born Merwan Sheriar Irani in 1894, in Poona, India, into a Zoroastrian family of Persian origin. While attending college in Poona he was attracted to an ancient woman named Babajan who lived her days seated beneath a certain tree in the city. [Note 8 p. 136] She was recognized in India as a perfected spiritual being, or Perfect Master - one who has completed the process of evolution through myriad forms and human incarnations to reach a stage beyond the gross, subtle and mental cages that bind the rest of us to the world.

A series of contacts between 1913 and 1915 with five Perfect Masters in all, led to Merwan's revelation of His true nature and destiny as a Perfect One, and ultimately as the Avatar of this age. The 'Avatar' denotes the Being who is distinct from all saints and yogis and gurus, however perfected they may be. As opposed to a Perfect Master, or Sadguru, who is essentially 'man become God', the Avatar is 'God become man'.[1] This is the descent of God in human form, known in mystical traditions as 'The Ancient One'. It is He who has returned every seven to fourteen hundred years in the form (in our present cycle) of Zoroaster, Rama, Krishna, Buddha, Jesus, Mohammed and now Meher Baba. However, He was known and revered as a Sadguru for much of His life and only unequivocally revealed His true identity (as Avatar) to the world in the early 1950s.

In 1922 he formed His own circle of close disciples who came to be called the 'mandali', and started to be called Meher Baba, meaning 'compassionate father'. In 1925 He began His silence, which was to last the rest of His physical life. Thereafter He communicated with the use of an alphabet board, and from 1954 onwards exclusively with His own system of hand signs, which certain of His mandali became adept at interpreting. Concerning His silence, His own words best convey its essence:

> *"I have come not to teach, but to awaken. Understand therefore that I lay down no precepts.*
>
> *Throughout eternity I have laid down principles and precepts, but mankind has ignored them. Man's inability to live God's words makes the Avatar's teaching a mockery. Instead of practising the compassion He taught, man has waged crusades in His name. Instead of living the humanity, purity and truth of His words, man has given way to hatred, greed and violence.*

Because man has been deaf to the principles and precepts laid down by God in the past, in this present Avataric form I observe silence. You have asked for and been given enough words - it is now time to live them."

With reference to the first words of this statement, Baba's self - designated role as 'Awakener' signified a departure from all previous Avataric cycles, in that He said He came not to establish a new religion, but rather to breathe new life into all of the world religions and to unite them "like beads on one string."

Meher Baba travelled extensively in Europe and the United States during the 1930s, contacting countless people, some of whom would be instrumental in spreading His name and carrying on His work in the West right up to the early 1990s, when the last of these early contacts passed away.

During the 1940s He travelled throughout India giving Darshan[2] to many thousands of his adherents, who came to be called His 'lovers', or 'Baba Lovers'. A notable feature of His work during this period was His contacting those He called the 'God Mad' or 'masts', distinguishing them emphatically from those who were mentally infirm or judged insane by the medical profession. These were in quite a different category. He said they were 'God intoxicated' and stuck in their journey towards God, from which predicament they needed releasing by a perfected being. He said, amongst other things, that these 'masts'[3], through the work He had done with them, would be of great benefit to mankind in future incarnations.

Of special note in his (visible) work in the West are two things. He created a Centre in His name in Myrtle Beach, South Carolina, USA which is to this day a place of pilgrimage, retreat and spiritual regeneration, and which He called His 'home in the West'. Secondly, in 1952, soon after visiting the Centre for the first time, he was in a car accident near Prague, Oklahoma. He said that this was entirely within His control, that it had to happen, and that His blood was to be spilled on American soil for the purpose of His inner work.

In 1956, He was in another car accident near Satara in India which held far graver consequences for His health and mobility. Again, He emphasized that this so-called accident was central to His work, as was the acute physical pain He experienced for the rest of His life.

In 1958 He inaugurated what was (with Meherabad[4] and the Myrtle Beach Centre) to be the third of the three places of pilgrimage in his name. This was Avatar's Abode, a couple of hours drive to the North of Brisbane in Australia.

No biography, however compressed, can end without mention of 'The New Life', a phase of Baba's work which took place between 1949 and 1952, and which He conducted as an example and a blueprint for the living of the spiritual life now and in the future. It emphasized a spirit of 'companionship' rather than hierarchy in the relationship between Master and disciple, which in turn implied more generally that the idea of any spiritual leader would came closer in meaning to that of a companion or 'elder brother'. This is best illustrated by some excerpts from '*Song Of The New Life*', written by Baba's close disciple Dr Ghani at His request:

> *There is no small or great now, for us all;*
> *The questions of disciple, Master or Godhead, no longer arise.*
>
> *Brotherliness or fellow feeling is the link that exists. ...*
> *This world or the next, hell or heaven, we no longer bother about. ...*
>
> *What has value for us now is to live in the active present.*

Baba appears to have been laying down an archetype for now and the future. One which would be typified by non-attachment to all and everything which hitherto has given mankind a sense of structure and orientation in the gross world. A breaking down of hierarchies, categories, comparisons and rankings. A kind of permanent positioning of the self on a threshold on which, as He said, we strive to live in a state of 'hopelessness and helplessness', relying only on God. Paradoxically, the *Song of the New Life* also states:

> *Dear ones, take seriously the words of Meher Baba when He says, "Although now I am on the same level as you all, Yet all orders from me, good, bad, extraordinary, You should carry out immediately, leaving the result to God."*

Meher Baba dropped His body on January 31 1969, and His tomb is at Meherabad, near the town of Ahmadnagar in India.

FOREWORD.

From 1969 until 1986 I was involved in all the groups and special projects that Michael's story recalls. In '86 I 'closed up shop' at 228 Hammersmith Grove London, where we lived in the apartment above Don, and returned, with my family, to Sydney, Australia. Later on I moved to Alice Springs in Central Australia.

This move may have been perplexing to many of my old Baba companions, but Don took the trouble to visit me there. I took him to Uluru (Ayers Rock) and other places off the beaten track, and Don cheerfully met (with deep appreciation and a sense of companionship) some distinguished and wily Aboriginal people with whom I am connected. Don caught a glimpse of the arduous realities of the life in which I was engaged. Some years ago I wrote an introduction to *Tales of the New Life with Meher Baba* narrated by several of the mandali who accompanied Baba, and edited, amongst others, by Don. I think Don understood when I hinted to him that perhaps this life in Alice was my version of living a phase of 'New Life' - in a stripped down, unromantic way. A life I never anticipated when we were in London.

This shift of my point of gravity also meant that I had no participation in the European and American events after 1986 that Michael describes so elegantly.

A Memoir of Don Stevens

Alas, not for me the seminars in Cagnes Sur Mer (I would have felt at home there), and not for me the ardor and arduousness of the 'Beads on a String' pilgrimages to avataric sites that Michael describes. (But I experienced, in compensation, some deftly luminous sacred sites of Central Australia.)

I went to London to visit Don in 2011 knowing he would not be long for this world. I arrived at Hammersmith Grove for our 12.00 appointment. Don had been taken that morning to hospital, and there he met his death. I was a day too late.

Don was, and is still, within the fibres of my being, a constant companion. And indeed, he was constantly, as Michael describes, 'a man of great heart'.

His account tracks this man as I knew him to be: playful, precise, businesslike, generously attentive, intuitive, indelibly imbued with Meher Baba - and ever forgiving.

This memoir is a tender story which also, between the lines, reveals Don's integrity and our uncertainties, our generation's naïvetiés and determination. We were so fortunate to fall into the company of Stevens, and of each other, and to catch the glance, the nazar of Meher at that crucial period.

Craig San Roque
27 March 2017
Alice Springs, Australia

PREFACE.

Michael Morice's *Meher Baba's Man in Europe* offers a glimpse of Don Stevens that might otherwise never have seen the light of day. Don's complete biography has yet to be published, but it will be, along with what I expect to be many more less ambitious but equally valuable remembrances of Don; and now they will face a very high bar in terms of accounts that are both enduringly meaningful and intimately personal.

I knew Don well myself, most particularly an "earlier Don" than Michael describes in this book, and as one of Meher Baba's non-resident intimate disciples he certainly deserves the central focus he occupies here. Though perhaps that statement needs editing even before its ink dries, inasmuch as for Don and for all who were close to him, Meher Baba was always and forever the only true "central focus" in Don Stevens' life.

In many ways Don was an enigma, even to his closest companions. He was at once a very normal and ordinary fellow and simultaneously an intimate of the Avatar of the Age. He was invariably practical and mind-swimmingly spiritual. He lived richly and enjoyed the world's gifts while at the same time his life was in many ways simpler than that of an ascetic. He was, in short, a disarmingly unusual combination of all these seemingly disparate and often opposing aspects in one human being.

I like Michael's story of his connection with and understanding of Don because it brought me closer to both of them. It is hard to imagine that anyone interested in Meher Baba and His Advent would not find this book fascinating; and it is impossible to think that anyone who knew Don would not enjoy and greatly appreciate this book.

Rick M. Chapman
27 July 2017

Meher Baba's Man In Europe

A Memoir of Don Stevens

Don Stevens, Cagnes-sur-Mer, France, 1980

INTRODUCTION.

This short memoir spans the period of Don Stevens' final 42 years in this world, in other words from the age of 50, his age when I first met him. At an early stage of writing, I realized I was remarkably ignorant about his first 50 years. During a long period in which I had ample opportunities I, by nature a curious person, somehow failed to ask him much about his life prior to my meeting him. Of course, this must have had much to do with the dynamics and the circumstances of our relationship.

Here, however, are the bare bones of Don's early history. He was born in 1919 in the State of Nevada, USA, and grew up in California in the region of Sacramento. He graduated from Johns Hopkins University in Baltimore in 1941 specializing in Organic Chemistry.

Attracted to mysticism from an early age, he met Rabia Martin either in his final months at university, or soon afterwards. She was the Murshida - spiritual head - of a Sufi order in California which she began in 1911 under the authority of the Indian Sufi Hazrat Inayat Khan. Rabia Martin separated from Khan's movement in 1930, several years after his death. Much later, in 1945, she put her Order under the guidance and authority of Meher Baba, never having met Him. Don was initiated into this Order, which came to be called 'Sufism Reoriented', and he became a senior person in the Sufi hierarchy in the years following Rabia Martin's passing, while Ivy Duce was the Murshida.

Don first met Baba in 1952, not at the Centre in Myrtle Beach, nor in California - where Baba was headed when He had His accident - but later that summer at Ivy Duce's apartment in New York City.

Mrs Duce's husband was high up in the oil business, and may well have been one of Don's main stepping stones into the profession in that industry that he pursued right up to retirement in the mid-1980s, ending up as a Vice-President (Europe) in the Chevron Oil Company.

During the 1950s and 1960s Don, by Baba's order, was co-editor with Ivy Duce of English language versions of the *Discourses* and *God Speaks*; and the author of a major book, mainly about his time with Baba in India in 1955, titled *Listen Humanity*. Medical problems had prevented him from attending the "three incredible weeks,"[3] involving a specially invited group of Western men, in 1954. However, perhaps as compensation, he was invited by Baba the following year as one of only two Westerners - Francis Brabazon was the other - to a large gathering of His Eastern lovers.

In 1968 Don was assigned by his oil company to Spain, and not long afterwards to England which was his principal base for the next few years. When he arrived in London he was still a senior member of

Sufism Reoriented (California USA). His subsequent relations with that organization were, it would now seem, only vaguely understood by the English Baba group. What is a fact is that not long after his arrival Don was no longer a member of Sufism Reoriented. He was generally known as a 'former Sufi' by the time I met him more than a year later, and that is where my story begins.

It is absolutely the opposite of exhaustive, at least as regards historical facts. My title - *A Memoir of Don Stevens* - implies a personal and often subjective vision of the man, while the events I describe are selective but, to the best of my ability, factually correct. Therefore I claim a certain accuracy as regards my own point of view, but leave yawning spaces to be filled by others, if they wish, with their own authentic accounts. And just as I knew so little about the Don of his first 50 years, so also I realize that many knew him far better than I during his final 20 years. In a way, this memoir is written from a distance in relation to Don's last years, with the hope of closing the gap that had opened up between us.

Along the way, readers may discern other possible, or probable, or partial, motives for writing about Don. Some are of a personal nature - personal to me at least - and some, you could say, come under the general heading of 'putting the record straight'.

Overall however, I believe I have a story to tell of general interest, about a remarkable man, towards whom I was prodded by the Avatar in the first fledgling weeks of my coming to Him.

I.
LONDON.

I first met Don Stevens in August 1969 when I was taken to my very first Baba meeting by my future first wife Barbara. This was at 87 Wardour Street in Soho, the early meeting place provided by Pete Townsend before there was an official Baba Centre in London. The street was mainly known for housing the offices of the film and music industries. For those unfamiliar with the place or the time that is being described, I should explain that Soho, in the centre of London (and incidentally the birthplace of the engraver, painter, poet and mystic William Blake in 1757), is made up of a web of narrow streets and alley ways, in which can be found a concentration of small restaurants and cafes with an international flavor, including the whole subsection of Chinatown. At that time we were seeing an explosion of clothing stores for the young on Carnaby Street and its environs. A thoughtful observer might have been tempted to speculate that the superficial efflorescence of colour and style was perhaps a sign of some kind of a shift at a deeper level. There were flared trousers with floral patterns for men, mini skirts for girls that had started off just above the knee but had shrunk with time to being nearer the size of cummerbunds; velvet suits for men, hot pants for women, high heeled boots for men, thigh boots for women, hats with wide floppy brims, and ruffled shirts with outsized collars for both sexes. There were tattoo parlors, antiquarian book stores, an extensive selection of strip-tease joints and sex shops as well as many of the famous West End theaters - and, of course, the ubiquitous pubs. Overall, the lighting was - and is - gaudy, with a dominance of the colour red, as befits the general tone of the district. Much of this description applies to this day, although the bookstores are sadly on the wane and the red light aspects less untidy, more sanitized and regulated.

The meeting place in Wardour Street was an upstairs studio flat. It consisted of a medium sized loft-like room with bare floorboards and large half-circle windows. There was a stack of chairs, a tiny kitchen and a bathroom. Most probably, the feeling of being in the swing of things - in the middle of 'swinging London' - was enhanced by the sensation of being in a former home of a superstar of the rock world. With all this in mind, I have a still fresh memory of my excitement as we went to the meeting, before I had ever set eyes on Don.

Here was a good looking dapper man about 50 years of age, dressed in a well - cut pinstripe suit, with neatly parted hair and a beautiful sonorous voice. For the whole meeting he expanded with fluent elegance and much authority on a chapter of Meher Baba's *Discourses*.

I sat entranced, invaded by a sense of recognition, whether of the man or of what he was talking about, I am not sure, but perhaps both; also by a sense of love. I didn't formally meet Don until the meeting was over, but even as he sat facing a very full room, I had the feeling he was talking to me personally, as if no one else were there, though I expect this feeling might have been shared by many of those in the room.

I cannot remember if I had actually by then 'come to Baba'. Almost to the day a year before this, I had had a profound experience of love, which had followed a moment of deepest despair. Despite knowing about Baba, I had not at the time seen this as coming from Him. However, with this in the immediate background of my experience, I think that, in the time leading up to meeting Don, I really was a bit of a sitting duck as far as falling for Baba was concerned. Especially so once I met Barbara who had recently returned from the 1969 Darshan in Poona [1]. She was fond of referring to a photo of Baba she had with her, a copy of the one that had occupied Baba's chair at the Darshan. One day, as I gazed at the picture, I recognized, or remembered, Him for who He was. When the time came, it was as simple as that. However, it happened in the context of what I can only describe as a storm of spiritual awakening that was raging at the time, and near the very centre of which, along with Delia De Leon[2] and Adi Jr., Baba's youngest brother, was Don

Stevens. The actual date of my coming to Baba, whether it happened before or after my meeting him, seems less important than the general atmosphere prevailing at the time, in which many besides myself were swept up, and in the context of which this meeting with Don took place in Wardour Street.

Not long after, Don invited Barbara and me out to dinner. We came up to his office in St James, which was situated close to the two main royal residences of the capital. It was directly behind Fortnum and Mason, famous for its up-market foodstuffs, and the Ritz Hotel; and adjacent to a street sporting purveyors of fine clothing to the nobility and the upper classes. As a location, this was about as high end as you could get, but in contrast to the surrounding opulence, Don's office was a simple affair. Since he was a high ranking oil company executive I had expected a battery of typewriters lined up on tables in a very long room, as befitted the oil industry in full swing. What we came into was a small ante chamber with room for one secretary with a desk, which gave on to another larger room with a desk, on which was a telephone, no visible paperwork, and facing it a couple of what I remember as rather sparse looking upright chairs. I had not yet come to see, as I would later, a lone telephone and no paperwork as an indication of status or corporate clout, so I didn't quite know what to make of this. What I did later notice was that Don, at least in his work for Baba, kept many things in his head which most of us kept on paper. He had little use for diaries and calendars and rolodexes, preferring to keep a reminder of things to do and people to call written on a piece of plain, expendable paper which he kept folded in the inside pocket of his jacket. He absolutely must have had an address book with telephone numbers somewhere, though I never saw it, and of course there was a secretary who will have kept the workings and appointments of his day job up to date and squared away for him.

Barbara and I sat down facing Don, who came round from his side of the desk with his chair to join us. Then he asked me quite flatly and without ceremony to give an account of myself. This was startling: a situation that put me on my mettle and totally disarmed me all at the same time. I can think of at least three things that Don may have achieved by putting me in the spotlight like this, whether he consciously intended to or not. Firstly, he gained an idea of me for himself; secondly, he gave Barbara a chance to see more objectively if she was putting her money on the right horse; thirdly, I was able to hear myself say unexpected and surprising things about myself that gave me a whole new tolerance for the direction my life had so far taken, and even the beginnings of a deeper understanding as well. Here, I should explain that I believed I had very little of substance to report. I had spent the previous winter and spring living in a fairly remote place in the mediterranean region, smoking a large amount of cannabis, and trying between smokes to get in touch with my creative self, mainly through writing. I had so far in my life failed to get a regular job, go to university or do the legal training which my parents wanted me to do. I was sticking obstinately to the belief that once I had an idea of what life was for, I would get up and do something, even devote myself to a cause, but that until that time arrived I saw no point in doing anything in particular. In hindsight I would say that a mixture of angry self-destructive rebellion and sincere existential angst were about equally balanced. My parents at best saw me as a bit of a lotus-eater, at worst they wrung their hands in sheer desperation.

I had an interest in spirituality. I was convinced that God did exist, but up to then my convictions had been fed by the books I had read, and had not really come alive as things to be lived in everyday life. My search for a spiritual teacher was casual to say the least. That winter my friend Sebastian had written me from England to tell me that Meher Baba had passed away, and my initial feeling was one of relief. Now I could strike Him off the list of contenders for my attention, and I decided that Sebastian must have chosen the wrong guru.

My conspicuous lack of attainment formed a large part of the self-image that I brought with me into Don's office that evening. I remember thinking that I was well and truly in a spot with nowhere to hide, and that the only course open to me was to give the most honest picture possible, warts and all. Early on in my self - exposition, I began to sense that Don was not particularly interested in external accomplishments, of which, in any case, there were so few. He seemed to be showing an interest, not in the bare facts, but in what was really going on all those years at another less obvious level. I did not mention the cannabis, my honesty didn't stretch to that, although he may have guessed; but neither did I mention my experience the previous year of 'love in the depths of despair'. That was something I did not, or could not, talk about to anyone other than my wives for many years. At some point I heard Don say, with great generosity, that I was someone who had been tracing an internal path, but that there had to be a balance with the external, and that we were here to deepen our relationship with Baba largely through action in everyday life. He suggested that I look seriously into doing a university degree, without which many interesting doors would remain closed. Further details have faded with time - all except for two: the sense of being wholly accepted as I was, and the sense of a great weight lifting away from me, along with the feeling that I had at last arrived, however tenuously, on the world's stage.

Then finally, following my examination, with the wind in our sails and full of good cheer, Don wined and dined us at Wheelers, a fish restaurant off the Haymarket, the first of the lubricated meals that came at regular intervals over the next few years.

Home for Don at this time and up to the mid 1970s was a spacious flat in the salubrity of South Kensington, furnished with quiet good taste, sporting a grand piano and some stunning original paintings on the walls, with only the odd discreetly placed photo or two of Baba, which you had to search for if you were not familiar with the place. The one small framed photo of Baba that I do clearly remember hung opposite the door to the guest bathroom at the end of a hallway. I wondered if a more open display of Baba's image on the walls might have raised too many eyebrows belonging to visiting denizens of the oil industry, although of course they will have been hard put to miss the one I have mentioned.

Here, on social occasions, as also in his later homes, Don liked to let things flow, in more ways than one. There would be a blatant gleam in his eye as he poured you an outsized Scotch whiskey 'just to start things off,' and several were the times that some of us neared our limit, or went beyond it.

The dual aspects of teacher and companion threaded our earlier relationship, with the 'teacher/mentor' uppermost at first, and the 'companion' gaining as I (and others) became more relaxed around him. I noticed that Don sometimes mentioned the word 'friendship' in his relationship with members of our group, and I had the impression that this denoted something that he valued very highly indeed. Given Don's background with Baba, and with the Sufi tradition, the meaning of the word 'friend' and of the word 'companion' would have carried for him a certain weight that for the time being and for some time to come would have been lost on the rest of us. And perhaps he already intuitively perceived the deep internal links that he possessed with each of us (and we with each other?) as 'friends'.[3]

At the practical level it was easy enough to see, as the years went by, that he was increasingly aware of the whole business of teacher/mentor versus companion/friend, perhaps especially in light of the fact that, while he was a born teacher, he remained aware that he was still only a bridge for us to the true Teacher-Awakener, Meher Baba. Unlike the latter, Don didn't always get the balance just right; it seemed to me that this was a coalface at which he worked very hard. Viewed from a distance, it would seem that his plying us with whisky and good food was most probably an integral part of this work. Under those conditions any sense of awkwardness or over-cramping respect tended to dissolve rather fast. On a lighter note, quite apart from any intentions Don might have had in feeding us, it has to be said that gastronomic pleasure in general was quite a feature at all times throughout his life. While apparently freer than most of us from worldly objects of desire, he made up for this in his enjoyment of whiskey, wine and fine food, most especially French cheeses picked up in his travels, washed down with a decent red wine, and the odd piece of English Stilton thrown in from time to time.

A Memoir of Don Stevens

To add to that of 'bon viveur', another feature that endeared him to me early on was the fact that he was a dog lover. Don occasionally mentioned a dog ('Denny') he had owned once in the distant past, which he had dearly loved. In one of his books he even made the observation that the dogs and cats of the latter years of his life were quite unlike those of his youth. He doesn't elaborate, but presumably he means that they, along with the rest of the higher animals, including humans, had already had a major 'push' from the Avatar.

At a more earthly level, there is a dog episode concerning Don which occurred in connection with one belonging to me and Barbara. This was a Jack Russell terrier named Aslan. He came with Barbara into our marriage, was well known in the immediate neighborhood, and was something of a character. He could occasionally be seen riding on the open platform of the milkman's van, doing a round with him in the morning before being delivered back to our front door. Most male dogs were not 'fixed' in those days, at least not in England, and he was known for his partiality to female dogs: the police had once called to tell us he had been picked up several miles from home on the A316, one of the main roads out of South West London, pursuing a German Shepherd and attempting conjugal relations with her.

As a housewarming present for the outsized, though ridiculously cheap, flat that we had managed to rent in time for the birth of our daughter Mani, Don had paid for the painting of the cavernous hallway and passages. One day he came to see the result. We had chosen a darkish lilac blue to cover everything, including the ceilings, and Don just stood rooted to the spot and speechless for quite a long time. We then led him into the future bedroom which we were decorating in a sumptuous shade of smoky ruby red below the picture rail, and a strong 'architect's' green above, ceiling included. The colour of Don's face was beginning to match some of the colours on the walls, and prospects for a convivial evening were not looking good, until Aslan apparently decided to take the matter in hand. Rushing into the empty room with a solid rubber ball in his mouth, he proceeded to throw it repeatedly against the walls with great force and then catch it expertly in mid air as it bounced around the room. Unusual though this dog was in several ways, quite apart from his name, I hadn't seen such a performance from him up till then. Filled with amazement, at last Don spoke, something along the lines of a whispered "well I'll be....." and the walls were forgotten, the moment defused, and life went on. In the seven or so more years that Aslan was in this world, Don rarely missed asking after him whenever we got together for a drink or a meal. Of course, he knew exactly how to warm me up with a dog inquiry to get a conversation going, but all the same, in his moment of glory, Aslan had apparently installed himself quite deeply in

Don's affections, and become a small feature in the background of our relationship, the agent of a bonding between dog lovers, so to speak.

***

Early Baba meetings at Wardour Street were attended by most of the young people from the London area who had come to Baba in the late 60s. As we went into the 70s and started to meet at the Ecclestone Square Centre, loaned by Pete Townsend's wife Karen, a group of regular attenders at Don's *Discourse* meetings started to form and meet separately in what was to begin with called the '*God Speaks* Group.'[4]

In contrast to the *Discourse* meetings, which were open to anyone, attendance at the *God Speaks* Group was by Don's invitation only (although I think if you asked, he tended to say yes.) This was the beginning of a closed group that met weekly or fortnightly for nearly 15 years, still known as the '*God Speaks* Group' at the outset, but which came in time to be called the 'Monday Night Group'.

When I use the collective 'we', I don't have a set list of names in my mind: in earlier times there was Michael Da Costa who left to live in Norwich; Dudley Edwards and Martin and Christine Cook; Sebastian Baker and Dallas and Barbara Amos who all left for California before we moved to Hammersmith Grove; Janet Judson (at that time Janet Podmore) who left in the mid-70s for India. There were others who came or went whom I have unfortunately forgotten; others such as Michael and Elspeth Milburn (who would drive up from Cornwall) and Maxine Summers, who were there at the beginning but not at the end; David Lee was there at the end but not at the beginning; and others I remember as being there from beginning to end, such as Craig and Georgina San Roque, John Horder, Molly Eve, and the Lees, Ian and Jan. These last two did leave before the end but I remember them as solid members for most of the Hammersmith years. I shall try to avoid the mistake of speaking for everyone when I should just be speaking for myself, and when I do use the collective 'we' I shall be trying to convey perceptions that, rightly or wrongly, I felt were shared, though not necessarily by everyone without exception. And, no doubt, each of those I have mentioned will have their own story to tell, similar in parts to mine, and quite different in others.

Once under way, the group incurred, amongst other things, the apparent disapproval and criticism of Delia De Leon for its supposed 'secretiveness' and 'intellectual approach' to Baba. This formed the core of Delia's long standing complaint against Don in an 'opposition' manufactured, for all we knew, by Baba for the generation of the energy He required for His work. Delia for her part upheld the artistic, freeform, unstructured approach to Baba. She had been an actress and had even owned, along with her family, a theatre in Kew where she lived, and theatre in its various forms was her forte. She did her work for Baba largely through parties and soirees and musical gatherings, and through a liberal use of the telephone on which she rarely announced herself, and absolutely never said goodbye before hanging up with a crash of the phone.

Don, diplomat that he was, would greet Delia with a mixture of warmth and courtesy, although he knew that behind the scenes she was not averse to stirring the pot of controversy.

Don did have at least one natural ally in his relations with Delia. This was Hilde Halpern, who had met Baba in California in the 1950s. She, a German speaking Czechoslovakian, was married to Otto, a Viennese nuclear physicist: they had both been rescued by the Americans from likely extinction, being Jewish, just at the start of the war, and whisked away to the United States. A psychoanalytically minded graphologist who had consulted to some of the rich and famous of Hollywood, she had come from Los Angeles with her family to live in London about the same time as Don (how adroit and compassionate is Baba's timing), and since she was an outsider and a newcomer, and a lover of most things American, we might surmise that the stage was set for an easy friendship with him. However, she also got along extremely well with Delia. She was another prolific and intrepid user of the telephone, matching Delia for vigour and panache in the use of that instrument. They rarely saw one another, but the lines were by all accounts kept very warm with their calls to each other in those early days, and it's fairly certain that one of the beneficiaries of their conversations was Don, who was known to be having, for a time, a weekly meeting with Hilde. This helped me, and perhaps others new to Baba's fold who knew and were friendly with all three of them. Knowing that some oil was being poured on troubled waters, that a potential rift was being contained if not healed, reassured me that the 'grown-ups' in Baba's London family were working in a common framework, if not hand in hand.

Among those who were reportedly less welcoming of Don was Baba's youngest brother Adi, who had lived in London since the mid-50s. Through the late 60s up to about 1971 Adi was a central pillar of the new movement, holding an open house on the first Monday of the month at which delicious Indian food cooked by his wife, Franey, would be served, followed by music, readings, tape recordings of bhajans and ghazals, and other entertainments. There we also met and became friends with Franey's and Adi's daughter Shireen, then still a schoolgirl, and with his son Dara and young wife Amrit.

I knew nothing, and still know next to nothing, about the specifics of Don's and Adi's personal relationship. However, I would guess that there might have been the natural tendency for some eyebrows being raised (and not just Adi's) towards a newcomer who threatened to upset the status quo.

A little more context here may be helpful. Those living in the London area, besides Adi and Delia, had included Charles Purdom who passed away in 1965; still going strong were Fred Marks, Tom and Dorothy Hopkinson, Molly Eve and her daughter Ann, and a few others of their generation who had met Baba at least once (and please note, none of these latter five were openly antithetical to Don, and Molly was a staunch member of our group). For some years they had formed a tiny band which had wondered how, and when, and if, a new wave of Baba's lovers would come on the scene. They had their answer one day in 1967 when a small bunch of scruffy young artistic types burst in on their meeting, asking "Is this the right place for Meher Baba?"

They were the vanguard, and over the next 12 months a wave of young people began to turn up and meet in the area of Kew and Richmond and Barnes in South West London, orchestrated mainly by Delia and Adi. They were followed only months later by the wave from the USA which was Don, offering structured classes on the *Discourses* and *God Speaks* to the whole of this new crowd! The situation probably wasn't helped by the knowledge that he had been, and perhaps still was, a 'preceptor' quite high up in the Sufi hierarchy in California, and that his imagined 'formal' teaching methods might be largely unchanged. To call this situation a bit of a turf war would not be demeaning those involved: after all that would have been entirely in keeping with the way Baba worked.

I have one vivid memory which cuts across the controversy, at least as it concerns Don and Adi. On the 31st of January 1970 on the first anniversary of Baba's dropping His body, the entombment film[5] was shown at the new London Baba Centre in Ecclestone Square. When it came to an end, there was a spontaneous silence lasting several minutes. It was filled, no doubt with sadness and grief, but surely also with wonder at the mystery of what had taken place one year before. Adi and Don both looked transported - and devastated. By design or by chance, like sleepwalkers they somehow found their way towards each other, and gave each other a long and heartfelt embrace.

Was I the only person watching? Am I the only one remembering? I doubt both of these things, but I know that the scene is engraved in my mind with a clarity and an immediacy in which the crowd around them has vanished, and in which 45 - odd years have collapsed into a timeless present. It's hard to exaggerate the significance of this scene for me. I felt a strong affection for both these men that I had known a mere six months. Until now I had never seen them together (and would never see them together again). The expressions on their faces impressed upon me their love for Baba - and Baba's love for them; and at the same time the power and the

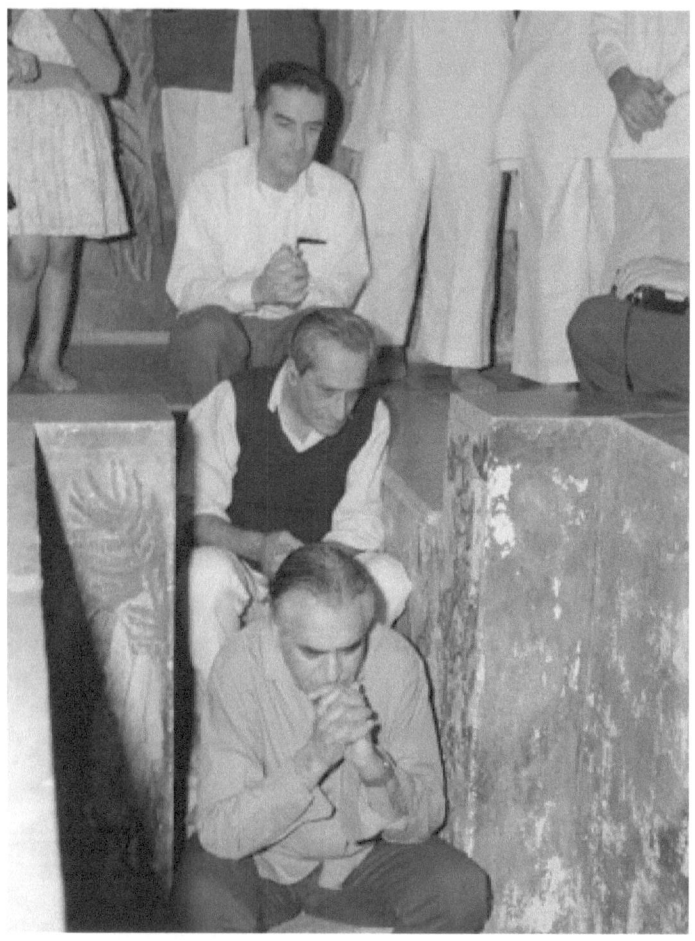

Adi Jr., Meher Baba's youngest brother, front,
Don Stevens top stair.
Meher Baba's entombment Feb. 1969

majesty of the occasion we had just witnessed that was known henceforth as 'Amartithi'.

The sight of them embracing was enough to convince me that these two men were as one when it came down to what was most important in life. After this I didn't pay much attention to the reports of a division between them, and was only reminded in later years of Adi's apparent disapproval.

Notwithstanding the evidence of what I have just described, there was a visible divergence of loyalties in the London Group one year or so into my being part of it. Adi, Delia and Don rarely, if ever, saw each other after the early 70s. The large number of attenders at Don's Discourse meetings began to diminish, leaving a core of people that stayed loyal to him for many years. Others veered towards Delia. Yet others adhered to Adi, such that I scarcely knew of their existence. That said, neither Delia nor Adi ever turned away a member of one of Don's groups, and many or even most of the latter had a friendly, or even a close and loving relationship with either or both of them.

So what was all the fuss about? With the benefit of hindsight through long distance binoculars, it really does look like a confection whipped up by Baba. Much of the antagonism was actually embedded in a past that most of us newcomers knew nothing about whatsoever: it involved the conflicting winds of personal relationships going back even to

A Memoir of Don Stevens

Harry Kenmore, Don Stevens
and Delia DeLeon in Tomb Feb. 1969

years before some of us were born. and that Baba alone understood in their entirety.

Concerning Don, we might only dimly and gradually have become aware that controversy and Don were familiar with each other. He seemed by nature to be a controversial figure and would prove to be so for the rest of his life.

Of immediate relevance was the life that he had just left behind, in which, as we believed, he had resigned his membership of Sufism Reoriented [6] and in the wake of which he had arrived in England. With reference to the remark I made two paragraphs back about the possible impact of Don's Sufi background on the elders of the London Group, there was a story that was doing the rounds, although never from Don in my hearing. In San Francisco under the authority of his Murshida, Ivy Duce, he had wanted to start a Sufi group in London attached to Sufism Reoriented in California. Mrs Duce had disagreed, precipitating , as we thought, Don's exit from the Order. I was pretty sure even then that this was the outer shell of a much more intricate story, but one about which I knew nothing until the very late stages of writing this essay. In a recent conversation with Laurent Weichberger I learned that Don had told him late in his life that he did not leave Sufism Reoriented of his own accord but was expelled following a full meeting of the membership in California, and without his knowledge, not long after he had come to the UK.

A Memoir of Don Stevens

Nariman Dadachanji, Sadashiv Patil, Eruch Jessawala,
Don Stevens, Upper Meherabad Feb. 1969

He learned the news from a fellow Sufi and personal friend - Ned Foote - who had himself resigned in protest at the decision taken without Don's having the chance to defend himself. Ned had then taken the trouble to come all the way to London to let Don know what had taken place. I also learned that Don had not only felt deeply hurt by the decision but had spent the rest of his life hoping to be reinstated.

As to the officially stated reasons for the expulsion, while Don may have heard these from Ned, they were not given directly to Laurent. Therefore, aside from further research with Sufism Reoriented, we will have to wait for history to unfold in its own time and way.

Not a word of this did he ever, to my knowledge, breathe to any of us. Hearing the story in retrospect colours my memory of those years in ways that are difficult to describe: I think my main emotion is one of admiration of the restraint and sheer poise with which he carried himself all those years. To know of this episode in his life is to be reminded that he must have had spiritual and emotional roots buried deeper within his identity as a Sufi than I ever realized at the time. This must have reached back, in this life at least, to his close relationship with Murshida Martin in the 1940s.

How could we possibly have assumed, as I think I did, that just because it didn't appear to have ruffled the surface of the face that Don presented to us and the world, this had been an 'easy break'? At the very least, Don was being faithful to Baba's wish put so memorably in *Song of the New Life* : "Even though your heart be cut to bits, let a smile be on your lips,"

Knowing now that this was a painful burden for Don, I hope that there was someone with whom he could have talked, if only to have help in digesting the indigestible. That 'someone', if indeed there was someone, might have been Hilde Halpern, Don's Viennese friend mentioned earlier, with whom he had for a time a weekly meeting. However, this is mere surmise.

On a rather less speculative basis, I wonder if, just as Meher Baba will undoubtedly have been behind Don's move to Europe, so also He engineered his break with the Sufis for reasons personal to Don, and reasons pertinent to His future plans for Don in Europe. Basically, there is a sense in this story that Baba wanted Don for himself, untrammeled by his Sufi ties. If so, I would guess thatBaba was using the personal susceptibilities of all the actors in this particular drama to bring about the result that he wanted. In which case, it seems a waste of time to attach any blame to any of the parties involved.

And lastly, another surmise in the form of a question: was Don's boundless energy and the freedom from worry that he radiated, something that was released in its abundance by the personal cataclysm that was his expulsion from the Sufi order?

At a more mundane level, something of immediate import for all of us who attended his groups over the years was the fact that Don was not under pressure to recruit us into the Sufi Order and we were under no pressure to join. We were able to take each other as we found each other, no strings attached, and that was surely all to the good. Two or three members of the early group did in fact leave England to join the Sufis, but that was on the basis of their own personal decisions, at least as far as I know.

And that is where I will leave this no doubt intriguing topic, along with (for now at least) the issues surrounding Don's 'controversiality'. In 1969 most of us knew little or nothing of all of this, and anyway, the vibrant present in those days left little room or inclination for dwelling on the past.

What do I mean by this? Although I have already described something of the spiritual excitement of arriving in Baba's force field at that time, I think it's worth putting in the context of the 1960s. Many nostalgic and idealizing things are still written and said about this decade, but it has to be said that a social revolution *was* taking place. In the UK it was sweeping away, or at least shaking up, a whole set of values and usages, to do with concepts of authority, empire, class structure, censorship, capital punishment, abortion, sexual relations including gay rights, dress, language and artistic expression, to name some of the more obvious things. The old dispensation had appeared to survive from the nineteenth century until well past the 1950s, though WW1 is generally said to have started the shift. For a younger generation brought up in the quite dreary and repressive shadow of the war years, it was really a time of great hope, and for many the true revolution was a spiritual one.

Speaking for myself, I remember feeling quite a lot of turmoil and confusion which no doubt came mainly from my own vulnerabilities, but was also surely due to the pace of change around me that my strict and formal upbringing and education in boarding schools had really not prepared me for. But then, in finding Meher Baba, I remember equally feeling that the whole purpose of being brought up in the way I had been, and of living through these uncomfortable times, had been achieved. That every step, or misstep, had somehow been necessary to bring me to that point.

So here was that vibrant present in which Don Stevens was destined to play a very special part. He brought a sense of Baba's energy that was like a strong wind that concentrated many hearts and minds, and persuaded us that, with respect to our aim and direction in life, we were right on target, even riding the crest of a wave.

***

Before I met Don, I remember trying to picture a bit of a nonconformist who carried the esoteric credentials of Sufism, but who at the same time was a corporate man high up in the oil industry—to my eyes quite a weird hybrid that attracted my curiosity. The idea of a Vice President of a major oil company conjured up in my mind one quite negative stereotype of a conventional, stuffy, authoritarian type. Sufism, a subject that was fashionable in a certain ambience of late 60s London, conjured up quite another, something verging on the exotic. I had dipped into the writings of the great Sufi Inayat Khan, amongst others, but was unable to find something in them that really connected with me. Continuing in ignorance, I had a picture of Sufism in my mind that was something closer to an image of whirling dervishes. Don the real person, as opposed to my two-dimensional polarized images of him, was much more interesting.

In about 1975, Don bought his flat in 228 Hammersmith Grove, not now his principal home, which was in the South of France, but intended as his London pied a terre. And from this time, meetings of the so-called '*God Speaks* /Monday Night Group' transferred to the room so many have come to know and remember with affection. This room stayed virtually unchanged in its furnishings and decoration throughout the rest of Don's long life, but its atmosphere, imbued with a sense of Baba's presence, grew from year to year. The furniture was comfortable and unremarkable, the carpet and curtains were of a 1930s art deco design, were never changed and eventually looked quite sorry for themselves. But overall, the flat was in stark contrast to the worldly sophistication of the Kensington flat, and seeing it for the first time gave me a quite exhilarating shock. It was as if Don had broken free of the ties of formality that had anchored him all of his life up until then, and that he was revealing a side of himself that had something of the wild in it. Dominating absolutely everything, to the point of rendering everything else immaterial, were huge blown-up black and white photos of Baba on every wall, most especially memorable being the well known one of Him in Mahabaleshwar leaning back against a railing with a great canyon behind Him at the spot known as 'Arthur's Seat'. From this and several other pictures He looked down on a variety of visitors. These no longer included the previously mentioned denizens of the petrochemical industry, since his office had shifted away from London to Monaco. But they did include the not infrequent, unsuspecting guest or guests plucked by Don from who knows where, often knowing little or nothing of Meher Baba. On several occasions I was also a guest, gaining a glimpse of the variety of contacts that Don seemed to make wherever he went.

One of these was a dinner as late as the mid 1990s to which had been invited two extremely well bred English ladies of high social standing in the Borough of Richmond in which I lived, and whom Don hosted with canny detachment in regard to the decor, with no mention of Meher Baba. The ladies played their part, behaving as if they were in a familiar restaurant, presenting smooth unruffled countenances, never appearing to look to right or left, as if this were the most normal setting imaginable for a dinner party, which by worldly standards it definitely was not.

In thinking of the room, I remember Don speaking sometimes of the 'baraka' that imbued a place dedicated to the contemplation of God. 'Baraka' means 'blessing' in Hebrew and Arabic, and is associated with the 'spiritual power of a person, place or thing' (Webster's English Dictionary.) Don's living room in Hammersmith, in the opinion of many including myself was, and is, indeed highly blessed. He bequeathed this flat to the English Meher Baba Association, whose Centre had lain in the same building on the floor beneath for many years. I always hoped that when he was gone it would be used in the same spirit as before, though perhaps it was too much to expect the pictures and the carpet and the curtains and the paint job to remain in place for ever; and, in the way that so much of the external 'scaffolding' in Baba's world is dismantled in time, it was announced that the flat was to be sold to raise money for a new London Baba Centre elsewhere. However, in the time it has taken me to round off this memoir, quite the reverse has happened, and even as I insert this sentence, a new, enlarged Centre has just been opened on the same site, merging Don's flat with the old Centre below.

***

The group that coalesced around Don and which eventually met in this room lasted in its original form for some 15 years, acquiring a reputation in certain quarters, as already mentioned, for a supposed exclusivity and intellectual approach to Baba. True, the group was closed in the sense that no new member was admitted without the agreement, not just of Don, but eventually of everyone, so fantasies and projections and rumours in the world outside could easily take wing and circulate.

Much of this critical view came from an image of Don's perceived didacticism, for instance when giving a talk which was open to all comers. These were first hand opinions that needed to be treated with respect. I agreed with them up to a point, especially when Don seemed rushed, possibly on the hop between plane trips and professional assignments. On these occasions he could be noticeably less open ended in his style of speaking. He had a way of asking questions to which he already had an answer, which might come at the end of groping responses from the floor. The trouble was that these perceptions tended to be carried over by people into their view of what they assumed Don must be like in his semi-closed groups. Then, the criticism tended to be born out of a misunderstanding or ignorance of what was unfolding as time went on. And sometimes, presumably, good old-fashioned human prejudice must have played its part as well. The main thing was that Don became increasingly less rigid with a group as he got to know it better. The lubrications of whisky and wine with light-hearted dinners could be seen in time to be doing their job, on him as well as on us, and for some years our meetings were memorable for their relaxed and free-thinking atmosphere.

What we were up to was actually quite the opposite of 'intellectual'. The guiding theme was immensely practical: the practice of Baba's presence in our everyday lives. This included the elucidation of the meaning of 'don't worry, be happy', as an ongoing practice; the active use of Baba's concept of the 'provisional ego'; and the practice of 'forgetfulness' as explained in the supplement of *God Speaks* written by Dr Ghani[7], roughly the equivalent of Don's often used expression 'putting things on the back burner', having once surrendered a problem into Baba's safekeeping. On the subject of instituting Baba as our 'provisional ego' Don was extremely keen that we should say what was on our minds out loud to Baba, rather than just speaking to Him internally. This, at the very least, was a way of articulating what we wanted to say, though it went further than that, because it forced us to drag any reservations of thought or feeling out of hiding and into audible space. As a passage from the *Discourses* puts it, in this process of 'giving everything to Baba', the ego gets "*stripped of all content*".[8]

With Don, the emphasis was always on the practice rather than the level of accomplishment. He would stress that it was the repetition that was important, the trying over and over again to be more honest and more open with Baba in a way that eventually would ingrain the habit of remembrance, even in the most pressing of situations where there was little or no room to think or breathe. Closely allied to repetition was the concept of persistence, and Don was nothing if not doggedly one-pointed and persistent in everything he did. In connection with this, a conversation with him springs to mind. Early on in our relationship I remember once saying I couldn't see how I was ever going to climb the mountain (of life) confronting me. Don answered with a nautical analogy. "Have you ever seen an ocean liner or a giant tanker in harbor in a tight space? It has to be turned round to face the ocean in order to sail off. Just three or four little tug boats do the job. Over an extended period of time, they pull it and nudge it with the tiniest of movements until at last the enormous vessel is fully turned round and ready to leave." Don meant this in the most practical of ways relating to the execution of the daily tasks of life and career; by extension, the meaning of this for me came in time to be that the infinitesimal nudges and repetitions of the tugs were like the taking of the smallest and sometimes least likely of opportunities to make ourselves 'ocean ready'. To remember Baba while putting your best foot forward, despite multiple failures, in order to take the next tiny step towards Him.

What follows is a perhaps unusual illustration of the practice of remembrance in quite a pressing situation in a very 'tight space', of which I was reminded recently by my second wife Lisa. Coincidentally, it features a very large ship. Don was in a meeting of high-up oil executives and clients which involved the clinching of a deal contingent on the punctual arrival in port of a giant oil tanker. Things were not going well, and it seemed likely that a lucrative contract could be lost, at which point Don 'dropped' a file of papers on the floor beneath the table and bent down to retrieve them. While under the table, he told Baba the situation in a whisper and returned to the upright, we presume with a straight face. I don't know the subsequent timing, but all did turn out well. Such tales encouraged us to experiment in situations of our own, some of which we then would relate to the group.

The subject of criticism in relation to Don, mentioned above in connection with Delia and some others in the Baba world who did not attend his group[9], deserves some more space of its own. Over the years, many have been the times that I have found myself defending Don, and I presume that I'm not the only one doing so. Criticism came not only in terms of his so-called didactic and controlling approach, but also sometimes in terms of the sort of person he was thought to be in more general terms. Not exactly character slurs, but hard-knuckled opinions all the same. Towards the closing years of our group, even our own dealings with Don were not without their own pronounced vein of criticism, and that is something I shall come to later on in my story.

Criticism is something Don seemed to readily attract throughout his life, and on his own say-so he didn't like it. He was fond of telling the story from his stay with Baba in Meherabad[10] in 1955, that he has written about in in his book, *Listen Humanity*. His sensitivity to criticism had become such a sore point that, on that trip, he decided to consign it to the dhuni fire[11], lock stock and barrel. Not long after this, he had found himself pelted with a hail of criticism from all directions with an intensity he had never met before, such that he felt he had absolutely no choice but to surrender this vulnerability ever more deeply to Baba.

By the time we knew him he appeared to have his sense of hurt under pretty good control, at least in that he didn't show it and was able to comment on the criticism and even joke about it. Even more to the point, he occasionally referred to his own critical nature in days gone by, including the first years after coming to Baba. Most memorably, because it implied a criticism of Baba Himself, he used to talk about some of those westerners he saw in earlier days that were drawn to Baba, of whom Baba would make quite a public fuss. Don would feel bemused by this, since in his estimate many of them didn't seem to deserve it. He would talk about his bafflement at how Baba could have such "poor judgement" (sic) as to pick such "unpromising material" (sic). Needless to say, as time went by he was forced to eat his words as he saw these same people blossom into the wonderful human beings Baba knew they were from the beginning.

This lesson clearly was brought to bear in Don's dealings with much of the 'unpromising material' which was drawn to him in late 60s London. Many of us will have stories to tell of his unwavering belief in all that was best in each of us. Don was a businessman, but with a difference, in that his most significant investments of time, emotional support, attention to detail, and interest free loans were in the personal development of the young people around him, in whom he implicitly believed, often long before they believed in themselves.

Coupled to this was Don's sheer practicality when it came to dealing with the nuts and bolts of daily existence. From sleeplessness to financial insolvency to problems with your family, colleagues or your boss, he listened, and listened with interested concern. No matter what your woes or bugbears, he always seemed to come up with a perspective, sometimes quite unexpected, but most of the time quite to the point.

By way of conveying something of the essence of the practical side of Don, here is a story that possibly risks a descent to the ridiculous. It's an account, second hand but on good authority, of conversations Don is said to have had with two young Baba Lover acquaintances out in the world somewhere.

> First aspirant: "Don, everything here is getting so expensive, it's becoming harder and harder to make ends meet."
>
> Don (deadpan, in sonorous and respectful tones, after a pause for thought): "Well, George (made-up name), have you ever thought of getting a job?"
>
> Second aspirant: "Don, I'm feeling so tired these days, its hard to keep going."
>
> Don (after pause for thought, in similar tones to the above): "Well, Deborah (made-up name), have you ever thought of getting to bed before 12 o'clock at night?"

It may be worth recalling at this point that Don was born under the astrological sign of Capricorn, those under its influence being noted amongst other things for practicality, one pointedness, attention to detail and deep obstinacy.

Still on the subject of how Don came over as a person, there was the apparent anomaly that I have already mentioned: that of his image as a high flying executive in Big Oil on the one hand, and intimate devotee of the Avatar on the other. I no longer question his part in the oil industry. Since oil has been the source of energy that has brought the world together physically into one inseparable whole, it seems totally unsurprising that Baba would have His own man deeply involved in it[12]. Equally, one could argue that the debate about its future, given its contribution to global warming, will be one of the main things eventually drawing us together at another level if we want to preserve the planet as a place on which we can continue to exist.

However, in the early days many of us were prejudiced against big business as something we thought was frequently tinged with corruption. There was a generally held view that Big Oil supported right wing dictatorships, and here in Don after all was one of its august representatives. If we had any views on society or politics, I believe they mainly went—of course with exceptions—in the direction of anti-authoritarianism and armchair anarchism, and some of us had only quite recently set aside a view of life through psychedelically tinted spectacles.

A Memoir of Don Stevens

Don liked to challenge our purity of principle with (by implication) the example he himself, among others, offered of a corporate businessman with integrity. He also insisted that the integrity of all or most of his colleagues at his level was beyond reproach. This we were prepared to believe, while doubting that this was true of Big business as a whole. His argument from personal experience was hard to refute; however, I'm talking of a time when most of us were of an age at which an affectionate irreverence for Don was liable to creep into the conversation about him in his absence. In the service of which, the subject of politics was easier ground for skepticism.

I heard it once said in a light hearted tone (I don't remember who said it, it might even have been me) that Don's politics were "to the right of Atilla the Hun." Of course this went too far, and was in doubtful taste; but perhaps it spoke of our difficulty in marrying our experience of Don as a compassionate and impeccable human being, with our shock at the occasional, though rare, throwaway remark he would sometimes make about some aspect of world politics. Occasionally, his stated off-the-cuff opinions didn't appear to be based on any sense of justice or spiritual high-mindedness that I could believe in. They seemed, rather, to be fixed views related to his upbringing, choice of profession or political affiliations. Certainly they formed part and parcel of the complexity of the man, but I came to see that they were really more a part of the superstructure of his personality rather than indicative of anything more profound. For me this was a lesson in the fact that social and political views are no more a reflection of the state of a person's heart and soul than is, say, his or her sexual orientation. At the same time, remembering a few examples of what I'm talking about fills out a picture of the man with all his contradictions that we came to know and love.

For instance, he once said to me that the Shah of Iran's only real mistake - leaving aside his torture chambers and his deadly secret police - was that he tried to modernize his country too quickly, so inviting the forces of reaction that we see to this day.

The UK Thatcher government's invasion of the Falkland Islands, to take them back from Argentina, represented "a much needed reinstatement of international morality." We knew enough about Argentinian politics to be able to distinguish between the oppressed ordinary people of Argentina, and its murderous military government; but at the time, patriotic fervor for Her Majesty's old fashioned imperial gunboat intervention was riding high in the country at large, and Don's opinion brought forth a gush of clamorous jingoistic anti-junta agreement from many of us.

Jumping down, now, a level or two - he once made a remark that I was not present to hear first hand but am pretty sure would have invited equally clamorous disagreement from most of us: that Mohammed Ali was wrong to refuse to fight in Vietnam because, regardless of his political views, obeying the draft was a due he owed as a citizen to society while others were paying with their lives.

And, jumping down yet another few levels, I was wrong to be living with Barbara (pre the cavernous flat) in a squat overlooking Kew Gardens. Don was apparently not aware that, in those times, moving into empty houses without renting or buying them first was considered by some to be an ethical way of solving the acute shortage, then as now, of affordable housing for young people in London. As far as he was concerned, Barbara and I were getting something for nothing, and that was wrong, even though I am sure I explained to him that the owner (a developer) had given his provisional agreement to our being there. This house, by the way, was quite by chance next door to Delia De Leon's residence, and needless to say *she* was delighted. This was not because of her instinctive opposition to Don in most things other than their shared devotion to Meher Baba. She would not have known his views on our housing arrangements; but her whole approach to life was nothing if not spontaneous and warmly emotional, regardless of the strictly ethical rightness or wrongness of a situation. So, merely knowing Barbara and I were so close at hand gave her great joy.

I cannot remember exactly how long it took me to realize (perhaps I even knew it all along) that Don, while conventional and conservative to a T in some respects on the outside, was quite the opposite on the inside. And this observation didn't take into account the room where we met which defied the rules of conventional worldly decor; nor did it take into account the external evidence of Don's lifelong use of his spare time spent in the service of an oriental guru; nor the intriguing anomaly of 'the sufi - or rather the sufi apostate - in the pinstripe suit'.

A little scratching below the surface of first impressions reminded me that Don's understanding of human psychology, justice and destiny started and ended with a fundamental insistence on the drop soul's existence from caveman to self-conscious God-loving being and beyond, rather than on the span of a single human life. These subjects had little meaning for him outside of this perspective. For instance, the Darwinian theory of evolution came up for occasional discussion in the context of my undergraduate studies. Don considered this theory wrong, arguing that just because all phenomena of life are related to apparently random organic processes and reactions on the basis of survival of the fittest, it didn't follow that they were intrinsically 'caused' by these processes. "Correlation does not mean causation," he might have said. This was not because he believed in the creationists' teaching that the world was made in seven days (God forbid), but because, as he pointed out, evolution was not random but purposive; the purpose in question being the drop soul's mission to know itself consciously as God after countless incarnations on earth. Thus, in its drive to achieve full consciousness in the human form, it was consciousness itself that drove evolution, rather than the other way round.

From these first principles flowed various unwaveringly held views founded on the karmic law of cause and effect; the belief that for everything we did we had to pay; or, to put it another way, every action or experience on our part had to be balanced by one that was its equal and its opposite, before the final goal, the knowledge of the Self, could be reached.

One striking example of this view in action would be Don's attitude to the question of capital punishment. I never heard him state an open opinion about this but I inferred his view from one or two things he said in relation to various articles in the news. I hope I am not misrepresenting him when I say he had no problem with the murderer paying with his life, not for the purpose of revenge or even for the protection of society, but because it saved him the trouble of having to come back to face the music in a future life.

And now to give a view of another side of Don that appeared to contradict his more straight-laced conservatism: on the subject of sex and relationships, Don - while frowning on risqué sexual jokes - was a liberal, or at least highly practical and pragmatic. His attitudes and advice tended to run counter to the leanings of any young 1960s bohemian types who might be attempting to follow to the letter Baba's instructions as-per-the-*Discourses* -Volume-One-Chapter-19. In other words, practising premarital sexual abstinence and not having a very good time at all. From what I could tell, there appeared to be a consensus in the older Baba community on the subject of Baba's discourses on sex and marriage. The main message coming from that direction was that these discourses were given to mankind now and in the future as the unwavering standard for those who aspired to come close to God. Meanwhile we, as we set out on our journeys in this life with Baba, should be careful not to impose these standards on our lives, chapter and verse, before we were really ready for the act of obedience they implied. That did not mean that we need not take them deeply to heart and hold them as a standard to be aspired to, and worked towards with time; but we might be missing the spirit of Baba's words, and the whole point of learning from experience in our present lives, if we treated these discourses as a rulebook to be taken literally at the outset.

Don, in harmony here with Delia and others of their generation who had met Baba, while certainly discouraging promiscuity, was mainly interested in the quality of love in a relationship. He encouraged marriage if practical circumstances and emotional readiness allowed it, but he was also deeply supportive of anyone pursuing a relationship in a sincere and heartfelt way, in or out of marriage. Regarding married life, older Baba people, including Don, thought we were unwise, going on mad, to eschew contraception too soon and leave ourselves open to responsibilities and decisions that we may not have been ready for. In this, as in many things, he was much kinder to young people than they were to themselves. And he did once say to me that if we battened down too tightly on our instinct to get into a close relationship with someone - for supposedly 'spiritual' reasons - then we were in danger of missing out on the richness of experience that could ripen into wisdom in later years.

Apropos 'richness of experience', and 'wisdom', one may ask what life experiences Don himself brought to bear in his work with us. His homosexual orientation was not something that was acceptable to all in the wider Baba community. Some mentioned it in tones that implied their surprise that one of Baba's main men should be anything other than a straight up and down solid family man. Perhaps we should remember that in the 1960s and -70s homosexuality in western society was only just emerging from the shadow of illegality. Centuries of social and religious views on the subject had shaped the law and were, in their turn, in accordance with it. All, or most, of the reactions I'm alluding to came from sincere people who would gradually come to the understanding that sexual orientation made not a jot of difference to Baba's estimation of an individual.

Don himself could be quite exasperated at what he referred to as reports getting back to him about his "sex life", which he implied were wildly exaggerated and appeared to have come as complete news to him. He told us in the group (perhaps by way of allaying our curiosity) that sex, at least in the present, held no interest or relevance for him. From this, I and others I knew well inferred he was a 'non-practising homosexual', if he was anything at all. Perhaps at the time we wanted to make it all sound more acceptable to ourselves and others. No doubt, though we probably considered ourselves to be emancipated liberals in this department, those of us who carried the label marked 'heterosexual' did still think deep down that we were the 'normal' ones. Now I think that this question matters, and mattered, not at all; that the important thing was that Don had, in the past and/or in the present, emotional attachments to men or to women. Of those in the past, some he may have looked back on as mistakes or with sorrow or regret, others he may have remembered with fondness and pleasure. Whether any of these included a physical relationship rests in the domain of Don's private life. The important thing is that all this 'richness of experience' was surely necessary to the broad sense of tolerance and compassion and wisdom he brought to bear in his dealings with our cohort of young people, who were themselves drawn from the wider spectrum of sexual orientations. These were his family, in the deepest sense of the word.

A Memoir of Don Stevens
***

When it comes to giving a coherent summary of Don's views on human psychology[13] - still under the overall umbrella of his supposed 'conservative' attitudes - many thoughts come to mind since I myself was a student of psychoanalytical child psychotherapy following my undergraduate years, financially subsidized at first by Don. Some of his observations seemed to be quite judgmental, but turned out on reflection to have been made out of care and concern. There was the time that he remarked that psychotherapy applied to children must be sheer torture for them. Actually, some of the interpretations recommended by the fundamentalist branch of the psychoanalytical profession did make my hair stand on end; however, balancing this was my belief at the time that child psychotherapy was tantamount to the holy grail, so at first I was quite put out. I could have agreed that in the wrong hands what he said must certainly be true. However, as I considered myself to be on the side of angels, coming to give relief and sustenance to the oppressed, backed by my gold-plated training, I stayed rooted to the spot, unable to make him explain more clearly what he meant. Don probably wanted me to be more mindful and circumspect about the business I was getting into. He most certainly approved of what I was doing, and without hesitation had loaned me the money for my personal analysis, which the training required. However, he might have known that learning to gauge and respect patients' limits of understanding, or their tolerance of some truth about themselves, did not come easily. Only a small part came from formal teaching. The greater part came through experience, hard work, and a liberal dose of humility about your own limitations and the limitations of your profession. Of course, if I was ever looking for a short cut to the stemming of overweening pride in my profession, all I had to do was go to India. At Meherabad and Meherazad, a psychologist could meet with total indifference to the announcement of what he did for a living. To claim to be one quite understandably cut no mustard whatsoever in the home of the one and only true Psychologist!

Back in England on the more gradual track I was treading with Don, the hints came more gently, leading, amongst other things, to a cordially shared agreement that the young were especially vulnerable to the ministrations of an overzealous therapist. It's worth adding here, a propos of all this, that Craig San Roque who wrote a foreword to this essay, has also written[13] to say that Don had seen a therapist or two in his own childhood or adolescence, and that his views on child therapy, both positive and negative, might well have come from personal experience.

I once made a remark that Don seemed to imply was not just self - indulgent, but also plain wrong. I happened to mention that I presumed my childhood had a bearing on whatever present difficulties I had. Don was too polite (and kind) to contradict me openly, but the expression on his face spoke for him. I was quite hurt: here was a man, on the one hand my benefactor, but who on the other, appeared not to care about the trials and tribulations of my early years. However, I was confronted with the evidence that a man who seemed to be saying 'you reap what you sow, don't blame your parents or your upbringing, there are no extenuating circumstances.' could also be deeply understanding and compassionate. When I come to think of it, Don absolutely never made any allusion to, nor showed any apparent interest in, anyone's childhood, whether happy, sad or indifferent. His focus was always totally on the present. And, as a counterpoint to what I've just said, a memory comes to mind of Don more than once acknowledging with painful concern his awareness of the estrangement of so many young people from their families. This was one of the downsides, albeit perhaps necessary, of the 1960s 'revolution' that I referred to earlier. In my close observation of young people and their families in later years, I would say that the estrangement was never again so deep or so widespread.

Putting the stories above in context, Don's views on psychoanalysis, thrown in my general direction as was his way (see below), began to come to the fore as his views on Darwinian evolution and related subjects took a back seat. He and I had a running dialogue, verging on friendly argument, lasting several years, which never really reached a conclusion, mainly because it seemed he was fond of firing a broadside at me just as one or other of us were leaving the room in bit of a hurry. Echoing the example of my personal experience given above, he would pick on the fact that Freudian theory was based on a view of character and personality built on infancy and childhood in a single lifetime - this life being, from the point of view of Freud et al, the only one we had.

In answer to Don's sallies on the thresholds of doorways, I would try to say that things were not so cut and dried, and that anyway I wasn't a Freudian except in the most general sense. I would counter with the news - implying he was a bit out of date - that modern psychoanalysis had moved on from the central importance of recall of early experiences. It was now based much more on the understanding of the relationship between patient and therapist in the here and now. This practice was enshrined for me in one famous quotation by the eminent psychoanalyst Wilfred Bion. He had, incidentally, treated Minta, Delia's sister, for a number of years after she stopped seeing Baba, so presumably knew something about Him. The quote from him was about the importance of 'eschewing memory and desire'[14]: memory of what had gone before in the patient's life and treatment; and desire for a particular outcome; in other words, the necessity of living completely in the present in the room with the patient. In the context of my dialogue with Don, this line of argument gave me the satisfaction of at least giving him pause for thought, if not exactly halting him in his tracks, but the debate had no particular outcome, other than keeping me thoughtfully aware of a broader perspective.

I wasn't impervious to Don's hit and run tactics, probably affected as much by the fact of the person using them as by what he was actually saying. In terms of theory, for most of my thirty years of professional life I felt like a bit of an outsider looking in - and out - from the margins of the profession. At times I lacked a sense of direction or was becalmed by a lack of theoretical conviction. Alongside working with children and adolescents, I did a further (exhausting) training in psychotherapy with adults, partly to relieve the exhaustion of working exclusively with children. This was a natural extension of the work I was already doing, and therefore greatly interested me. However I found I always had a much more solid and spontaneous feel for practice (as opposed to theory) with children and young people. And that was where I felt Don's unwavering support.

***

If asked to highlight Don's 'internal qualities', as opposed to his external 'Big Oil right wing rigidity', I would settle for this one attribute: his belief that most people were intrinsically good and decent, and that treating them as such brought out the best in them. It was his way of grasping much of your essence while paradoxically accepting you just as you appeared to be on the outside. Of course, this essence was ultimately the recognition of God in all of us. Coming down to earth, you could say it was the very thing that gave us back a more heightened sense of self-respect and self-love. This is not to say that Don's insistence in seeing the best in everyone didn't land him in trouble from time to time. I've heard it said that he was not always a great judge of people. From a worldly point of view, he seemed to have a bit of a blind spot in various situations. I can think of two notable instances in which a financial swindle of sizable proportions appeared to be the result of Don's choice of a suspect entrepreneur. Equally striking was Don's insistence in defending his man to the last, ever willing to allow extenuating circumstances to sway him towards leniency. This was infuriating for those who, with Don, were at the receiving end of such scams. For some it reinforced the view of Don the rigid control freak, unwilling to admit his mistake in a situation that had clearly run away from him.

Don's controlling nature was in my experience one of the main characteristics upon which his critics would seize. It's worth expanding on, particularly as it's highly relevant to an episode that changed the nature of my own relationship with him for good, and which was probably relevant to the eventual breaking up of our group.

In our Monday Night group, a situation evolved in which Don progressively encouraged us to take more responsibility for the direction of the group and, by implication, to depend less and less on his leadership. The new order that he had in mind was intimately tied up with the ideas of 'inner links' and ' Companionship'.

The use of the term 'inner links' comes from Baba, whose last message using his alphabet board in 1954 included the following:

> *"Severance of external relationships does not mean the termination of internal links. It was only for establishing the internal connections that the external contacts have been maintained until now. The time has now come for being bound in the chain of internal connections"*.

'Inner links' and their fostering was not felt by us to be a problem. I think we expected them to be forming and strengthening by Baba's grace and by dint of the time and effort we had been putting into our meetings over such a long period of time. The latter term 'companionship' at least inasmuch as it referred to our relationship with Don, presented more of a challenge. It comes from one of the central ideas of Baba's New Life (see my preface and footnote) in which a hierarchical relationship between

Master and disciple is replaced with one in which we relate instead to an 'elder brother'[9], a first among equals, who is at the same time a fellow companion on the 'same level' as us. I cannot remember him ever talking specifically about this. However, I took it that Don felt that the example that Baba offered as 'elder brother' in the New Life was one to be put into action in his own groups, in which he himself acted, ideally, as 'elder brother' in a non-hierarchical group.

I'm not sure when the ideas of inner links and companionship found their way into the discourse of the group; probably quite gradually, until eventually they seemed to occur naturally in much of what we talked about. However, despite the aim of companionship and 'equality', it was often apparent that Don was still in charge in such a way that our would-be emerging independence could feel undermined. To be honest, we were collusive in all of this in that we were naturally ambivalent about 'growing up'. But at the same time, we were face to face with Don's own struggle to relinquish control. This made for a painfully awkward atmosphere in what was to be the closing year or more of the life of the group. For some time we seemed to work hard without apparently getting anywhere. Don was also working as hard as anyone, but we could see how difficult it was for him to step out of the driver's seat, which was his avowed aim. Once, things almost came to a head: angry feelings about how he continued to make us feel controlled, while professing to want us to take more responsibility, were simmering away just below the surface and were close to erupting into the open. However, the hostility was somehow sublimated or diverted, I can't remember exactly how, other than the fact that we managed to control ourselves. Don put this in a generous and positive light: he felt that our more murderous instincts - to deal him a hammer blow and consign the group to the dustbin - had been withheld from action, much to our credit and, more importantly, to our (spiritual and psychological) benefit!

In the context of our group, Don must certainly have been aware that he had to elude all attempts to put him on a pedestal, since he was just the bridge for us on our journey towards the one and only Master, Meher Baba. Even so, the whole process of establishing Companionship, along with deepening of inner links, as the main modus vivendi of our meetings was, as we have seen, an elusive thing. As I've already suggested, it could be argued that the push and pull between Don and the group ended in its breakup; for me it ended in a personal 'break' with him which at the time was painful, and entirely unplanned. To describe this process, which happened in parallel with the 'elder brother' project I've been describing, I need to go back a few steps to give a bit more context.

Don was too polite to say it outright, but I'm pretty sure he had a low opinion (verging on despair) of the business acumen of most members of the group. This would have been an accurate assessment: relatively well versed in the arts and literature, we mostly didn't have much of a clue when it came to handling money—our household budgets, yes, but in the realm of bigger money I believe Don thought we were space cadets, dismally equipped to deal in the kind of Baba work out in the world that he increasingly felt to be of great importance. To this end he set about training up some of us through participation in one of his projects, in which we also served a practical purpose. Various of us, at various times, thus became members of the board of a charitable company, 'In Company With Meher Baba.', with which he had no formal or legal connection. Don had set up this entity to channel tax free donations, largely his own at the outset, towards selected Baba projects around the world. At the beginning, this most especially included donations toward the setting up and equipping of a hospital at Meherabad. I was not one of the first to be asked by Don to be involved, but eventually my turn came.

While the board of 'In Company' had only an indirect connection to our London group, one of the disconcerting factors was that in our final year, time was increasingly being eaten into by 'In Company' business talk, at the expense of what we thought to be the real task. This was one of the ways whereby Don, having apparently made progress toward relinquishing control, would reassume it in the way described a little way back. As one can imagine, when we discussed business Don was well and truly back in command while we tended to sink into passivity, and at times became impatient and put out. In contrast to the timeless pace of spiritual considerations, business decisions apparently had to be put into acton without the slightest delay. I remember my heart sinking when I heard Don say, for what seemed the umpteenth time, "now on this, speed is key..." when the mere effort of getting to a meeting at the end of a day's work seemed hard enough.

In November 1985 I attended an Annual General Meeting in the US at which various direction-changing decisions were made. The company came out of the AGM with a new name - 'Meher Fund'. A new constitution marginalized Don's ability to influence decisions regarding the allocation of monies. The new (American) chair in particular felt that we came close to being a laundering facility for Don's tax deductible financial activities - and, having seen a couple of recent examples in the press, he was adamant that he didn't want to go to jail! He was backed up by two attorneys on the board who brought the weight of the law to bear on the matter, and pressure was applied for a unanimous vote. In fact it was made clear that only a unanimous vote would do. I was shocked at the apparent all-pervasiveness of what was being proposed. Of all the members of the board, I believe I was the one most personally beholden to Don, in several ways. He no longer loaned me money - although I still owed him plenty - as I had been qualified and self-financing for several years. However, I had an ongoing association with him based on regular meetings, gratitude and a deepening friendship. I wriggled and squirmed and spluttered, but frankly I was too green and new to the game to be able to go on resisting, and eventually - faced with the logic of the argument - I agreed, not just to abstain, but to cast my vote with the rest.

Following this, I was the designated, perhaps even the self-designated, conveyor of news to Don back in London that was not at all to his liking. I think that in the throes of his first reaction Don took what I had to tell him as a personal betrayal. It was the closest I would ever see him coming to anger —and anger with me at that. What I saw was an instantaneous clamp on any verbal utterance. A shutter came down almost visibly over his face, but not too soon for the emotional affect to reach me full blast. I felt like a messenger summarily shot at point blank range; in fact I was not just the messenger, I was party to a business decision that had pressing legal reasons, but which was made independently of him and without warning, so that it came as a major shock, and an implied rebuke. I believe the thinking at the AGM was that if we sat down to talk about it all with Don, he would manage to talk us out of it!

And now, knowing a little more about the nature of Don's exit from Sufism Reoriented, I feel it's impossible to avoid another way of viewing the impact of the decision taken at our Board Meeting: a meeting at which Don was not present just as he was not present at the Sufism Reoriented meeting which expelled him from the Order. At least in its outward trappings our decision in 1985 bore an uncanny resemblance to that taken by Sufism Reoriented to expel Don back in the 1968. Both decisions presumably carried their own separate weights of betrayal (from Don's point of view). However, I cannot help feeling that the news I had brought him must have stirred up memories and emotions of which I had no inkling. I wasn't just facing a reaction to a moderately intolerable piece of news causing passing anger and discomfort. Judging from Don's reaction I suspect that I was witnessing a detonation of something far deeper. I had gone to see him, as I naively hoped, in the spirit of a 'Ned Foote' but in fact, unlike Ned, I had not resigned from the Board in protest. I was representing the side that had pushed him out.

In the wake of my meeting with Don I tried to repair the breach with at least two letters explaining the thinking behind 'the decision', but each of these was replied to with a highly impersonal letter to the whole board. With the reception of Don's second letter, I remember feeling very upset, certainly, but also a bit peeved that Don was overreacting, and ought to be 'getting over it' (so little did I know). More realistically, I could see our closeness fading away with an inevitability that was putting it beyond our reach, though I hoped not for good. All in all, looking back, the whole business felt like a case of 'killing the father', in the psychological sense. Following that line however, one would need to add that for the long term mental health of the individuals concerned, the killed-off father eventually has to be revived and reinstated in a position of friendship, trust and respect vis a vis the 'sons', the perpetrators of the deed. The time I would have at my disposal to try to achieve this would be the roughly 25 years remaining to Don in this life.

Bearing this picture in mind, I think that the board meeting itself was a precipitating factor in the final break-up of the group not long after it took place. From that time on there was a distinct distancing between Don and ourselves, and the group seemed to dissolve of its own accord, with no formal ending that I can remember.

It would be superficial and rather wishful on my part if I said that the personal 'break' with Don was not really so serious at all, that the basis of our relationship was undamaged, and that, to paraphrase Baba's last message on his alphabet board (see above), the severance of the external relationship did not mean the termination of our internal links. This was a jarring experience and I've always been unsure of what Don thought of me in its wake, especially since at our less and less frequent meetings over the next few years he maintained a friendly but slightly detached air that seemed to say, amongst other things, that the subject was not necessarily over, but was off the table for discussion. With this in the background, for some years it was hard for us to feel much pleasure or relaxation in each other's company in the rare moments we were together. For one thing, we were both a little tongue-tied: there was no topic available, no work in progress, no point of reference that didn't seem forced.

With time the feelings I had about this threaten to fade from recollection. I find I have to dredge my mind and my conscience to summon up a more truthful, less window-dressed memory of how I felt. Anger was certainly in there at the beginning, along with a sense of annoyance, when I did see him, at some aspects of his public style of speaking. Generally, I felt a tendency to feel more critical of Don, though still ready to spring to his defense when I heard some of these same criticisms coming from others. Also, a sense of resignation began to settle in, resignation to the possibility that the distance between us would only grow greater with time. The gathering ice was eventually broken in an unexpected way.

In 1992 my mother died leaving me the money to be able to pay back Don's loan in full. We had not been closely counting the installments of fresh dollar notes in a plain envelope that he had been handing over to me on a regular basis for a number of years. He had told me once that I should only pay him back when I felt able to do so without seriously impoverishing myself, and that time might even be long after he had passed away.

I did a calculation on a piece of paper and wrote him with my estimate. Don replied saying that this was just about the amount he himself had in mind, and once he had received my cheque he wrote again to say that it had come just when it was needed to finance a certain project which otherwise would have been starved of liquid cash. From that time on I found that I faced Don with much less of a guilty sense of being in his debt while feeling I had been disloyal to him. I was even able to feel more of a positive kind of debt, which in turn paved the way for a renewed sense of gratitude. This is not to say that the fading whiff of mutual resentment didn't still hang in the air, asking for the assurance of mutual forgiveness, but I was able to see a way out of the mire if and when the opportunity presented itself.

Opportunities did come, though they were few and far apart. I had left London to live and work in North Devon in the Southwest of England for a few years from 1985. When I returned to London I became buried in my career, a new marriage and family concerns for quite a time. I seldom went to Baba meetings, including those where Don might have been present, for a longish space of time between the early 1990s and the early 2000s. As the years went by my sightings of Don were all too rare, although one happy consequence of the thawing of the frost between us was that we felt able to have the occasional visit. Don came a couple of times to my home in Ham, shared with Lisa, down the river Thames from Richmond; there was the occasional dinner at his flat (sometimes with the aforementioned baffled or insouciant guests,) or a meal at a nearby restaurant in Hammersmith. So, the rapprochement with Don that I hoped for took place ever so gradually, with what felt like great unspoken care on both our parts, and was still really a work in progress when he passed away in 2011.

Meher Baba's Man In Europe

A Memoir of Don Stevens

Don Stevens and Michael Morice, London 2003

II.
EUROPE.

Well before the mid-80s, Don's centre of gravity, his focus of work both temporal and spiritual, had shifted away from England towards France and, by extension, the rest of Western Europe. His main home since the mid-70s had been in Cagnes sur Mer on the Mediterranean coast not far from Nice, although he returned regularly to the London flat where we continued to meet until the group disbanded in the mid 1980s. From the time that he settled in France he had been in the process of collecting together and motivating groups of Baba Lovers all the way from Brittany in the north to Marseille in the south. And, through the 70s and early 80s, while his professional work base shifted from London to Monaco to Madrid, Don was engaged on a major piece of work as per Baba's instructions: the commissioning and financing and publication of translations of the *Discourses* and *God Speaks* into French and Spanish and eventually German.

While Don was busy on several fronts, it was not as if his theatres of operation existed in separate watertight compartments. He was keen on bringing all of his friends together, whether from the US, England, France or beyond. And, come to think of it, the various 'international' meetings around this time were prototypes of what was to come - the beginning of a major theme (maybe *the* major theme) in the rest of his life's work.

I particularly remember one such occasion in the early 80s, an international gathering at his flat in Cagnes sur Mer. I don't remember the theme for the weekend, but perhaps that was less important than the freedom and frankness of the discussion, much in the way that Don (despite his fabled didacticism) had encouraged over the years. It just so happened that there was a guest at this gathering named Meherjee, one of Baba's mandali. He sat in silence almost throughout, and when he was asked quite late in the day what he thought, he was brief, humble and to the point - "I have nothing to say, but all this is just words." As I remember it, this didn't come over as a wet blanket on the discussion, but rather as something that added a deepened thoughtfulness, and remembrance of Baba's silence.

During the time our group was still meeting, I visited Don several times in Domaine Du Loup, as his apartment building in Cagnes was called. One of these occasions stands out. Don offered me the use of his flat to stay in alone for about a week over one New Year, to work on my final dissertation for qualification as a child psychotherapist. He and his friend Claude were to be in Argentina. Don had quite sternly inveighed upon me the need to be 'ruthless' with myself in the work at hand, but the brilliant Mediterranean light after the winter grey of London, and the intoxicating smell of cooking for the midday meal taken on a hundred French balconies facing the sea, meant that it took me quite some time to settle down. I had scarcely found something of a rhythm, and the required degree of ruthlessness, before Don and Claude returned several days early! That was the end of my work. Don despatched me by train the next day to Marseille to meet the Marseille Baba Lovers who were having a meeting, thereby introducing me to them, while giving himself some space to unpack and settle back in.

The remaining couple or so days until my flight home I spent with Don and Claude eating, drinking and watching TV. Occasionally Don would give an impromptu performance of classical music on his grand piano, reminding me that he had at one time considered a professional career but had decided he would never reach the standard required. This was a different and memorable view of Don. Accustomed to seeing him 'on', even to some extent when pouring the whiskey and hosting a dinner, here I saw him at his most domestic ease, letting Claude call most of the shots when it came to program selection and culinary decisions, and making me feel more like a family member than a guest. This was a special occasion, never to be repeated.

The 'Meherjee meeting' had come after this and was followed by a couple more visits with other members of the Monday Night Group. all within the time that it was still going strong, though after the time that Don had moved his base to France. Then had come 'the rift' and the break-up of the group, and for me Domaine Du Loup became a thing of the past. Don's base eventually shifted from the south of France to Madrid for a short time, and then to Paris, but one might have been excused for thinking he was in several European and American cities all at once, such was his level of activity; in my distant view galvanizing, initiating, cajoling, probably at times infuriating, individuals and groups right up to near the end of his long life.

By his closing years he had built a network of groups and individuals all the way across Europe from Spain to Croatia and Serbia and Turkey. In short, Don had become a major and ubiquitous catalyst in the quickening and deepening of Meher Baba's work in the West. And, to my eyes, he was becoming more and more a 'Frenchman' - if that can be said of someone who spoke French with such an atrocious accent. Atrocious not because it was 'American', but because of the blatant lack of effort at proper pronunciation, which went with a total lack of shame or embarrassment. We are talking here about a fluent French speaker living in France, but my impression was that the French found his way of speaking to be a source of enjoyment, even at times hilarity.

In August 2006, I had the chance to be a participant in the tumultuous activity I had been witnessing around Don from a distance: a 'seminar' had been scheduled in Marseille during my summer holiday. I had heard about these seminars sponsored by Don, taking place in diverse European settings. Although I had taken part in one or two earlier gatherings such as that attended by Meherjee and therefore had some foreknowledge, my view from a distance in later years had become a little skeptical: I had decided at some point that they sounded too dry and academic for my liking and therefore needed no further attention! Most probably this was an attitude left over from the critical opinions I had begun to harbour after our 'break' twenty years earlier; an attitude which up to now had stopped me, despite our gradual rapprochement, from really making an effort to reach out to Don. This time I took the plunge and booked a place.

The 'seminar' in Marseille was, for Don and a large group of companions, a stopping point on a tour on the "Beads" model (explained below) starting in Italy with visits to Assisi, Portofino and other places associated with Baba; then passing along the Mediterranean coast of France, to destinations in Spain such as the tomb of St Teresa at Avila. I was not prepared for the atmosphere of what you could call inspired chaos that greeted me, and which reigned throughout the four or five days. Here was a band of seekers in transit with its own built up momentum, in collision with a motley collection of seminar attenders carrying a diversity of mood, language, spiritual outlook and expectation.

Although international in composition, with a fair number of Americans and a sprinkling of attenders from Germany, Mexico and other countries, the main body was composed of British and French. My fellow countrymen as a group (of course with exceptions, but this is a broad brush) came across as a touch eccentric, with a talent for slapstick humour, sticking mainly to themselves, and with little French to oil the wheels of entente with the ancient enemy. Facing them were their hosts, with only a little more English than the English had French, apparently less eccentric, dealing with the invasion with an impressive show of Gallic *insouciance*.

The 'seminar' was composed of a series of presentations by people of several nationalities, with live translation into English or French, of artistic and literary and academic projects, directly or loosely or not at all (at least overtly) connected with Baba. In the course of proceedings, I noted with concern and embarrassment that the main body of English tended to vanish into thin air whenever someone French was on stage. Thoughts of 'perfidious Albion' raced through my head.[1] Was this, I wondered, the (perhaps unconscious) English reply to an imagined Frankish brush-off? And if so, which came first, and where and when had all this started? Was an ancient archetype, or stereotype, of behaviour between these two nations - one in which we ignored each other when we were not fighting wars - being enacted before our eyes? As for Don, it may not be going too far to surmise that he was not only aware of all of this but was reveling in the soup of many ingredients that was here being cooked up.

The lunch and coffee breaks that interspersed the scheduled events were themselves a study in the amazing atmosphere of chaotic energy, excitement and expectancy, that Don had apparently been building over the years, largely unbeknownst to me. Everywhere I went I seemed to see a huddle of travelers from Italy to Spain frantically trying to sort out the finances of the trip which seemed to have gone awry, with lists and receipts and balance sheets being counted and gone over again and again. My description here is no doubt an impressionistic one, coloured by the fact that I had been absent from Don's circle of influence for many years. However, what was a fact was the quiet, almost innocent, presence of Don in the midst of all of this, unfazed and unflappable, by now in his life quite bent over and ever smaller looking, but with undiminished strength of intellect, and great authority. Somehow, he had contrived a heady mix of seekers of God in an atmosphere replete with the presence of Meher Baba, with a distinctly European flavor. And this was appropriate, for after all Don had become, to my eyes at least, 'Baba's Man in Europe'.

A Memoir of Don Stevens

Eruch Jessawala and Don Stevens
in Mandali Hall, Meherazad, India, 1980

III.
BEADS ON A STRING.

The touring group I have just described, which was passing through Marseille en route from Italy to Spain, introduces a phenomenon which one could argue represented a final and crowning achievement: the epitome of Don's sense of practicality, intuition and sense of play in the invention of ways to bring people together in Baba's name, and for their own benefit and enjoyment. I'm referring to the "Beads on One String" tours, or "Beads Tours" for short, which took place in the early 2000s, three or four in total while Don was still alive, though he hoped they would be continued in some form after he was gone. The name of the tours refers to Baba's own statement that He had come to unite the religions of the world "*like beads on one string*".

They were initially conceived as group tours around India to certain places of spiritual significance, having their origin in the following sequence of events as recounted by Don.

Over a period of years in the 1950s Baba had told Don to go to various places (tombs of saints, temples etc.) in India, and to film them. No explanations were asked for nor given, and Don had resigned himself to never knowing Baba's intentions once Baba had dropped His body. Then one day not long before Eruch[1] passed away, Don learned from him that he had travelled with Baba incognito over the years to each and every one of these places, for reasons Eruch had never understood. This set off a powerful reaction in Don. His understanding, or rather his intuition then or later, was that these had to be places of immense importance in Baba's work, that Baba had left an "avataric powerhouse" in each of these spots for the future benefit of all who visited them [2]. When Don related all of this to some of his London companions, the overwhelming reaction was that they too would like to visit these places. And so was born the idea of taking a group of Baba lovers and other spiritually minded persons to these spots, seen now by Don as "storehouses of energy," that were variously associated with the Hindu, Muslim, Jain and Buddhist religions. At each site they would repeat the name of God appropriate to the religion associated with the place. As I understood this (rightly or wrongly) Don's idea here was in a sense to light the fuse to the charge that up to then may have lain dormant, awaiting just such a moment. Thus, participation in all of this carried the possibility that those taking part could have a sense of agency in Baba's work.

When I heard about the first tour, I was immediately curious and then excited. I have to admit that the idea of such a trip stirred the romantic in me. What came to mind for a fleeting moment was an image of Gurdjieff in *Meetings with Remarkable Men*, striding with his companions on stilts through a sandstorm in the Gobi Desert (in order to keep their heads above the level of the sand), 'in search of the miraculous'. Or, alternatively, of the company of seekers in Herman Hesse's *Journey to the East* [3].

Even if Baba were not involved, had never gone incognito with Eruch, had never sent Don to film, this would still have seemed such a creative and romantic idea on the part of Don! In the best manner of the literary legends whose writings I had read in the 60s before I came to Baba, here was the idea of a body of like minded people traveling together, admittedly with modern means of transport replacing stilts, with mystical intent. Later it did occur to me that much of my excitement was due to the prospect of traveling through a large chunk of India in Baba's footsteps. This idea has even more force in light of the privations of sleep, logistic nightmares and discomforts that traveling with Baba entailed, and a tiny taste of which we ourselves would be able to sample.

***

The Tour of January 2009 started in Delhi at a hotel deep in the car selling district of town, that escaped a label of dingy by just a small margin. Over 36 hours the party of more than 50 souls gathered from many parts of the world - India, France, the UK, the US, Mexico, Turkey, the Republic of Ireland; and perhaps some others that I have forgotten. Ages ranged from 18 to 80, with the majority between 30 and 60.

On the second evening, when all were gathered, we celebrated Don's 90th birthday in the hotel basement. By courtesy of English friends on the organizing committee who may have reckoned that I had known Don longer than most of the others had known him, I gave a speech to start things off. This was an unexpected honour for which I've been deeply grateful ever since, not least because I had the chance to say a few things along the lines of love and gratitude that I would probably never have been able to say directly to Don, if only because too many years had passed without our being closely in touch, and the intimacy was no longer there. Strangely though, saying something to Don in a rather public setting that I would not, or could not, have said in private, turned out to be what happened without my planning it, or even having the time to plan it. What a wonderful gift!

Some kind of champagne-like wine materialized from somewhere along with a cake bearing candles—though not to the number of 90—which Don was required to blow out. With much good humor and bubbling excitement and expectation, we appropriately marked the start of an adventure which for most, judging from the feedback, would turn out to be a highly significant milepost in their lives.

Over the next 2 weeks, starting in Delhi at the spot that marks the assassination of Mahatma

Ghandi followed by a visit to the Qutub Minar[4], with the tombs of Nizamuddin and Inayat Khan as a side trip, we travelled southwards by train and bus through Rajasthan. There we visited the tomb of Moinhuddin Chisti[5] in Ajmer, and the Dilwara Jain temple[6] at Mount Abu; then down through Bombay and Poona: Babajan's[7] tomb and 'seat' and Baba's L-shaped room[8] in His family's house with the well in the courtyard; on to Hyderabad to the 'Manonash' cave[9] in central India; back up through Satara, to the site of Baba's second car accident, and the field where he and some mandali had played cricket nearby; and the Rosewood bungalow in Satara itself where Baba gave up his use of the alphabet board in the course of an elaborate and powerful ceremony ; on up to Mahabaleshwar; Shivaji's fort[10] and the cave at Panchgani[11], and on to the Buddhist and Kailash[12] caves at Ellora; ending up at Meherabad the day before Amartithi 2009.

Several sites on this list(e.g, Manonash and Panchgani caves, the Poona sites and all the places around Satara) are directly related to Baba's own life and work. These sites were not amongst those visited in that special way by Baba with Eruch, and then later by Don, but were added to the itinerary at Don's suggestion because he considered them such powerful - and fresh - centers of raw spiritual energy waiting to be used in the unfolding avataric period. They were an extension of the original idea of the Beads on One String tours, and 'Parvardigar'[13] was the name of God repeated at each of them.

An added ingredient in all of this was that each site was researched in advance by one member of the party, who then gave a talk prior to the visit, or sometimes at the site itself. Having signed up late, I accepted the one place on the list still left to be researched and talked about: the Rosewood Bungalow in Satara. Thinking that it couldn't be of any special interest, since no one had yet volunteered, I wasn't very keen to begin with. My interest and excitement mounted, however, as I read about what had taken place there.

When the party reached Satara, no one knew the way to the house, but we had the phone number of the occupant. Due to an apparent blip in communications, this man was not expecting us, but he readily came to meet us on his scooter and led our bus to his home. As if in unquestioning submission to Baba's will, he and his wife welcomed our party into a crowded front room and stood with us while we repeated 'Pavardigar,' and listened to my talk in a language they did not understand.

The house itself exceeded all expectations. It was set back from the road in a sizable compound, pink rose colored on the outside as its name implies, and occupied by this elderly Baba Lover couple who, as far as one could see, had kept the inside exactly as it had been when Baba was there in the 1950s. The atmosphere so thick with the sense of Baba that you could have cut it with the proverbial knife. A totally unforgettable experience just to be there, let alone giving the talk in the room where Baba formally gave up His alphabet board in October 1954 - and delivered His famous quote about 'inner links', itself a theme so central to the whole point of the tour. The only thing missing was the presence of Don, who was presumably using the time to rest.

My mental pictures of Don from the tour are many and varied. Apart from some close conviviality and personal time we were able to have in Delhi, Don on tour was necessarily someone slightly apart. Without a doubt he was conserving his energy, much of which had to be put into his role as 'eminence grise' of the party. Sometimes, if staying at the same lodgings, he would address us all together in the evening after dinner, helping us above all to hold our focus on the idea of 'inner connectedness'. One of Don's guiding principles at this time - in the sense of being to my ears more explicit than in the past - was the concept of 'oneness,' its contemplation and practice. The main association of this word - oneness - in this context would be with Baba's 'beads on one string', most particularly in the sense that the latter phrase implied the breaking down of barriers between the world's religions.

However, it was also connected in his mind with the concept of 'the field', more accurately the scientific discovery of the so called 'Zero Point Field', an element of quantum physics. There was a book that Don was excited about - *The Field* [14] - in which the 'field' is described as 'an ocean of microscopic vibrations which appear to connect everything in the universe like some invisible web'. I was struck by the enthusiasm that a 90 year old could bring to a subject which in the wrong hands could have sounded dry and irrelevant. He didn't say much about it, but somehow managed to weave this idea quite unobtrusively into the fabric of the tour with a complete absence of scientific intellectualizing, making it possible for people to see its relevance to the original idea of 'Beads on One String'. I think it's no exaggeration to say that an enhanced feeling of connectedness really did begin to pervade the whole experience of the tour, helped, I believe, by the physical conditions, which no one had quite foreseen, and which I shall describe in due course.

Other than the above, Don seemed to pop up here or there in such a way that his appearance often came as a surprise. One of these appearances was at the tomb shrine of the Sufi Perfect Master Moinnudin Chishti, in Ajmer. This is the teeming and tumultuous site of Muslim pilgrimage which is considered by some to be second in importance in the Islamic world only to Mecca itself. Don was not with us on our arrival, although the tomb attendants knew him from a previous visit and clearly held him in great respect. Quite late in the day he showed up in a wheelchair, looking diminutive and even a little

Meher Baba's Man In Europe

passive and helpless, yet also strangely powerful. Regarding wheelchairs, there is this mixture of helplessness and powerfulness that those using them can emit, not forgetting for a moment the greatest exemplar of this, Meher Baba himself in his closing years! But this was the first time I had seen Don off his feet when he might have been on them; these days bent over ever more, but still mostly ambulant, while commanding an atmosphere of reverence as crowds opened up to let him pass. It seemed appropriate that this 'sufi' (Don) should be garlanded at the dargah of a realized sufi saint; and that a group of qawwali musicians should appear, as if from nowhere, to give him (and us) a rousing and unforgettable performance.

The other vivid picture I still have, helped by an actual photograph that I took at the time, is of Don sitting on a ledge in a corner of the Kailash Temple at Ellora on the last day of the tour. He was being filmed by the tour's own camera crew, so that a usually dark corner of the temple was lit up. There is a dynamic quality about Don which makes me forget his 90 years.

This may well also have been because here he had had a powerful experience when he had been sent by Baba all those years ago. Following Baba's orders, he went at night when the caves were closed, this time with Eruch accompanying him. He had gone in alone while Eruch, having persuaded the night watchman to let him take his place, waited outside. Don relates that he at first felt a growing presence in the darkness, and then a feeling of mounting, almost unbearable, pressure in his chest that subsided when he had rushed outside. Both Eruch, and later Baba, asked Don what had happened in the cave, but neither of them commented on his answer, and Baba had merely changed the subject. When Don brought his first Beads Tour here in 2004, he had had an identical experience in the same spot; and then the penny had dropped, and he had felt his intuitions concerning Baba's design were confirmed. He remembered that he had quite often had this same physical sensation, though less strongly, while in Baba's company. This convinced him that Baba was giving him a major sign of His continuing presence at the Kailash temple, as well as the intent of His previous visits incognito to the same places with Eruch.

At the time of our own visit I either didn't know this story, or else had forgotten that it took place here. Perhaps I was one of the few people out of the loop because, following the filming of Don on his own, many from the group sat around him, mainly in silence, and the atmosphere was intense. Looking at my photograph of this particular gathering, I find myself wondering at those faces free of any discernible expression, their awareness no doubt turned wholly inward. There appeared to be a field of energy around Don in those moments that was taking them out of so-called normal time and space. Something seemed to be going on that I was observing rather than really feeling part of. Certainly we must all have been feeling the effects - each in our own particular way - of two weeks of intense spirituality flavoured by the wear and tear of two weeks of logistic pressures and tribulations. Without a doubt, I myself felt 'smashed', to coin an esoteric term, and perhaps that's why I didn't really participate, and instead took many more pictures than usual as a way of just hanging on.

When I look at the photo of Don on his own I feel amazed at his resilience at the end of such a tour, and I ask myself what on earth kept him going. Seeing the reverence of ordinary Indians, and for a westerner at that, coupled with his clearly central place in the group, some skeptical outsider might be tempted to question the part Don's ego played in all of this. To him (or to her) I would want to say, "yes, Don's healthy ego may be involved, but it's one he has dedicated to Baba, who in that case will be making use of it for His own ends." Alternatively, one might say that he was a man inspired by an enormous sense of purpose; or even just a very tired old man putting one foot in front of the other, doing what he felt Baba wanted him to do, and dependent on Baba's support from moment to moment to keep him going.

A Memoir of Don Stevens

***

Readers may be comforted to know that Don, along with a few whose health didn't permit them the full rigours of the journey, did not go on buses and trains with the main party, but travelled in more comfort, often by plane, and managed to turn up on time at most of the sites.

This was just as well, since it became apparent early on that we, on the more arduous itinerary, were being 'gouged', to use Don's colourful term. The shabby quality of the hotels and restaurants that we had been booked into, along with the breakneck schedule that found us being tipped off trains in the middle of the night and loaded on to buses - or vice versa - affording broken sleep or no sleep at all, made it plain that the travel agent had skimmed the cream off the proceeds and trousered this along with his negotiated fee.

This all made for an interesting side-plot to the main object of the journey. One could even say that in time it became central to the main plot. We might have taken the view that the entrepreneur had done a brilliant organizational job, which was true in the sense that buses and trains, and hotel and restaurant stops, were efficiently calibrated, with everything running on time. And a great irony in all of this was that Don's man had managed to engineer a situation which gave us a taste of conditions on one of Baba's own tours with His mandali. For this we might have been grateful, but at the time the prevailing emotion felt towards him was that he had taken an enormous toll on our wallets and our goodwill!

The itinerary and logistics took on a life of their own, every bit as lively a feature as anything else in terms of its effect on the dynamics of the group. The entrepreneur and the travel arrangements and the dismal quality of food and hotels became a common enemy, weaving in with colds and chest infections and the relentless repetition of God's name in its various forms to induce a state of elated exhaustion and one-pointedness, and, for the most part, a state of amazing calm and oneness. It was even apparent that Franco - British relations, involving many from the Marseille event of 2006, had taken a marked turn for the better.

All in all, I would say that one of the main miracles of the tour was the way the members of the group coalesced around the physical and logistic difficulties, and presented an unruffled and united face to each other and to the world. Personal animosities and selfish foibles were for the most part invisible, if not entirely set aside. The contrasting and diverse backgrounds of the group yielded up their best in fortitude, patience, selflessness, good humour, sang froid and stiff upper lips. The band of travelers that arrived in a very dusty state at Meherabad just before Amartithi was such a close-knit unit that separating from each other to either go home or to merge with the tidal wave of humanity in full flow proved, from what I was told and what I experienced, to be an extremely difficult task.

Don Stevens, 92, being helped down the Kailash temple staircase, Ellora Caves complex, Beads pilgrimage 2010

I can see that the logistic side of the tour has already acquired a prominent place in my account. I think this must be because the physical journey itself, and the 'gouging', bore directly on our relations with Don. It was Don who had recommended the entrepreneurial individual who turned out not even to be an official travel agent, but merely the nephew of a friend, with little or no professional qualification for organizing such a tour. It was Don who, while acknowledging the ride we were being taken for, found every extenuating factor he could to get his man off the hook, ending with the theory that because he was engaged to be married and was short of funds, he more or less had to do what he did out of sheer necessity. It was almost as if he wanted us to accept this on the grounds that it was 'rational economic behavior'! What a show of loyalty when confronted by 50 stupefied travelers waking up later from the spell of the journey; what a show of the famous and infuriating Stevens Capricorn stubbornness - and, on tour, what a show of poise which played a major part in keeping the party on task when the scale of the swindle began to dawn. And finally, let us not forget the irony in the fact that Don had financed some of the travelers out of his own pocket in the form of a gift rather than a loan. From all reports, he was scrupulous in checking, in each and every case where he had a doubt, whether he owed these, and indeed others, any money. I do believe that Don intended to reimburse anyone at all who at the end of the day felt out of pocket or aggrieved.

I also was to have an exchange with Don along these lines - and it came in the following way. In view of the fact that the tour had been so demanding in various ways, it was perhaps not surprising that a noticeable number of participants had some kind of a crisis following the tour, often of a physical nature. My own crisis happened to be a heart attack that occurred very soon after arriving home, at a time and place that I was able to get the best possible treatment. Not long after, I received a phone call from Don which I at first thought would be for the purpose of commiseration and enquiry after my health. However, this didn't appear to be the case. Don passed rapidly over the heart attack, and came to the thing that was clearly on his mind, namely the finances of the tour and his earnest wish to know whether I felt I was owed anything: "Now Michael, " he asked emphatically, "do I owe you anything at all?" For me this was a clue to the fact that the tour 'gouging' actually continued to weigh on Don, perhaps long after most had moved on from it.

While I had no hesitation in telling him he owed me nothing at all, I think that another factor was also in play, one that I had noticed in Don from time to time over the years, namely the very careful keeping of his 'karmic accounts'. I think he wished to leave absolutely nothing behind in the way of an 'outstanding balance' if he could help it; absolutely the minimum that could be left in the gross world to come between him and his eventual coming to Baba. Regarding Don's question to me, I somehow doubt that a mere matter of dollars was all he was really asking about. I think he was far more concerned about any possible resentment or blame I might still be feeling towards him regarding the 'gouging'. In relation to that (the gouging) I could have happily said that I held nothing against him at all; however, on later reflection I realized we did have that 'karmic account' from deeper in the past that one could argue still needed to be settled. I could not know what, if anything, Don harbored about this in the deeper reaches of his mind, and even if the question had occurred to me, which it didn't, I don't think this would have been the right moment to ask him, dominated as it was with the recent pressing questions about the tour.

I saw Don twice more before he passed away in 2011. These were brief visits when we both happened to be in London, at his Hammersmith Grove flat where I think he still held meetings. The last time I was with him was about a year before he died, and he was there with Claude who was helping him clear out some personal effects, mainly books. It looked as if he was finally leaving for good, which was not the case, as a year later he returned and stayed here until he died in a nearby hospital. Don asked me to choose a book from a pile he was throwing out. I took a

Penguin edition of a book about Islam. As we talked, Claude staggered past the open door heavily burdened by a large cardboard box full of stuff. He stopped, his eyes darted a look of complicity towards me, and then he boomed in his inimitable way, "Don, when are you going to reTIEyeure....?? I think we all knew the answer. Don chuckled, and Claude continued on his way.

A few minutes later, I embraced Don as he stayed seated in his armchair and, bearing the book he had given me, I turned on the threshold of the doorway, the one that had seen those exchanges between us as one or other of us was leaving the room thirty or so years before, and we waved each other a silent farewell.

IV.
DON'S WRITING,
SOME REFLECTIONS.

I have come to a tricky point in the exercise, namely, one in which I would hope to draw things together and find something more 'profound' or 'essential' to say about Don than I have so far managed to impart. In the hope it may help me draw towards some conclusions, I want to devote the next few pages to talking about selections from Don's writing.

First of all, it's worth saying that writing as a creative activity was very important to Don, on his own say-so. I don't think it necessarily came easily to him, but some of his writing displays great vitality, and he probably enjoyed the challenge as much as anything.

I used to have a fairly fixed idea about the opaqueness of much of what he wrote, and partly for this reason avoided reading his books—but anyway, with Baba's own words to sustain us, and Don's availability in the flesh, what was the need? I still think that, especially in his more theoretical passages, some of his sentence structures reveal a man of extremely high IQ and spiritual intelligence, imparting ideas with a linguistic complexity that is hard for lesser mortals to follow on first or second reading. But to be fair, even if Don's writing when under his own steam may in some places have been dense and heavy going, when under the direct supervision of Baba, as in *Listen Humanity,* he wrote flowing English that was a pleasure to read.

Certainly *Listen Humanity* is one of my own all time favorite Baba books. Looking through it recently I found that some years ago, I had underlined several passages in the chapter titled 'Personal Relationships'. He talks about the courage and certainty he achieved through Baba to face things in life which previously would have sent him into hiding (p 206):

"... it may be that it is this complete acceptance of oneself which does it ... to feel complete acceptance by another human being is a wonderful thing. To find that someone has absolutely no negative reaction to the wrongness .... in one's life is worth more than all the gold in the world. It gives one courage to be one's real self and to risk whatever might come. The matter goes still further. It is not just acceptance by another person which does the trick, it's being connected with one's own inner resources as well".

This reminds me of how struck I often was by the sense of Don's fearlessness and his remarkable freedom from worry, which surely came from a very firm and secure internal relationship with Baba, giving him the courage to be himself and to take risks. He had schemes in motion, usually several at a time, some of which were risky to say the least, and which made it look at times as if he was 'flying by the seat of his pants,' as I sometimes used to think. On top of his regular meetings with groups, and the human responsibilities those entailed, mostly in France and England - and later the US - there was the launching of 'In Company With Meher Baba'; his European 'seminars'; the 'Beads' Tours in India and Europe; his later 'Young Peoples Groups' in the USA; and over an extended period of years, the financing and editing and publishing of the *Discourses* and *God Speaks* into several European languages, all the while writing and printing and publishing several books of his own.

Up to the mid 80s this all took place while holding down a high level job in the oil industry which itself, as he sometimes told us, often involved some financial tight rope walking: the resolution of last minute deals which, if they went wrong, threatened to rattle the wheels of some sizable portion of Western Capitalism, or so it seemed. As Don said to me once, action in the world consisted in 'doing the necessary,' basically making sure the nuts and bolts were all in place and properly tightened, "at which point, Michael, life becomes one heck of a ball game." The 'doing the necessary' was our part of the bargain, and the outcome was to be left in Baba's hands. His words, in particular the 'ball game' bit, captured my imagination because it carried a promise of the possibility of a freedom from worry, of a sheer enjoyment of life. Don's 'ball game' appeared to be one he played so well that, not forgetting his fascination described earlier with the ball game of the dog Aslan, he was able to have several balls in the air at once, and at the same time was able to communicate his own sense of enjoyment and freedom from fear.

Don's remark about Baba's complete acceptance of him as he was, and through this his being connected up with his own inner resources, is surely the key to understanding his attitude towards the people, and especially the young people, who came within his sphere of influence. His more critical nature, including his judgments of his fellow human beings, was well honed, as he occasionally hinted, by the time he came to Baba. So it would seem that being in touch with a special quality of loving acceptance came directly from Baba Himself, who opened up a priceless 'inner resource.' Thus we who were around him in the 1960s, 70s and 80s and beyond, were at the receiving end of something very special too. Rarely was a critical remark heard that was not couched in kindness; rarely a moment's anger that was not - if you looked closely - turned inwards with a slight darkening of the face and a blinking of the eyes. This is saying something when I remember how rudely he could be challenged in some of his talks, especially by audiences that included people who didn't know him. And our own poor self-discipline when he first knew us, for instance our lapses in attendance or our often poor time keeping, never once in my memory drew a sharp word from him. In fact, quite the opposite to what one may have expected, he never failed to greet anyone with less than a very warm "Hallo, so good to see you, come and sit down."

There was one exception that I knew of to this rule of kindness and tolerance, one class of people which did not appear to benefit from this inner discipline of his: namely, taxi drivers who overcharged, or took him 'the long way round', which comes to the same thing. Don had given up owning a car well before I knew him, and relied mainly on taxis for ground transport. It would seem that he considered taxi drivers to be a tricky bunch that needed a strong hand, that over the years he had got the measure of, and to whom he was pleased to deliver appropriate broadsides, either in English or in his singular brand of French!

To continue with the passage from *Listen Humanity*: Don goes even further in describing the "love, warmth and tenderness" he received from Baba. I found this passage moving, unexpectedly transparent for Don—especially in the way he admits his surprise:

> "First it (the love, warmth, tenderness) comes from Meher Baba, and one is momentarily caught unawares, perhaps even embarrassed by it. Then it comes from oneself, and again there is no anticipation of the action. It springs out suddenly where it is least expected, and one can feel something like a sheepish puppy which has unexpect-

edly wet in the middle of the living room rug, and now wonders whether it may have done the wrong thing...it is an odd fact of our civilization that people hunger for a lifetime for simple warmth, yet are afraid to show it and suspicious when it is offered... most people want it, most people look for it, most people are deeply touched when they find an honest trace of it, and yet few people are capable of giving it".

Judging by this passage, it's hard to resist the impression that Baba took the somewhat buttoned up scientist and gave him something well beyond what he may - or may not - have missed in the cradle: the pure milk of His own loving warmth and tenderness.

Apropos of all this, one of the most moving and heartfelt talks I ever heard Don give was in 2007, a few months before Lisa and I left England to live in the US. Don spent much of the talk describing a typical day with Baba at Meherazad, from being asked first thing if he had had a satisfactory bowel movement, to being administered one of Baba's special orange purgatives, to being taught with the lightest of touches an unforgettable lesson about Baba's idea of punctuality, and more. Here was Don in the aftermath of a very serious heart operation following an earlier Beads Tour, going back several times in the talk to the special kindness with which he had been treated in hospital - in such a way that it began to merge in one's mind with the tender treatment

Baba had extended to him on all of those precious days at Meherazad. Looking back to the previous paragraph, I think my use of the word 'cradle' may have been more apt than I realized: the hospital treatment, as well as the Meherazad treatment, feels as if it was extended in almost maternal fashion to body heart and mind - but especially heart!

And *heart* is really the crux of the matter. If I am managing to convey a picture of Don as a man of great heart, then I shall be quite pleased. He certainly wasn't just a cuddly teddy bear wallowing in a warm pool of affection, passing on to others the love and tenderness Baba had given him. Nor was he just a man of science and business driving some to distraction with his intellectual expositions on Baba and spirituality.

However, there is something else, a leavening factor, which I think needs bringing out a little more: his sense of play, and a quality related but not quite the same, his playfulness. These were always there from the start; in the gleam in his eye as he poured you a hefty whisky; in his appreciation of Aslan's ball playing skills; in his own view of life as 'one heck of a ball game' (once you had released control of the ball to Baba); in his wicked juxtaposition of society English ladies with outsize pictures of Baba looking down on them from the walls; in his conception of the European 'seminars' that brought certain national cultures and characteristics into a highly interesting play with each other; in his concoction of the idea of the Beads Tours, which were nothing if they were not enormous fun, besides being seminal, momentous and memorable.

And what of his writing? It is hard to characterize Don's writing as 'playful.' When looking for 'play' in the sense of the free play of his own thoughts and ideas, a good place to look would have been his *'Airplane Notes'*. These were originally hand written on loose paper, mainly, as their name implies, on his many plane trips in between our meetings in London, or in various hotels in major cities of Western Europe. Don would read them out to us at the start of a Monday Night meeting, and they typically contained thoughts that were still in the process of digestion, to do with themes we were working on in the group. Here are a few randomly chosen titles of entries which on average are a half to one typed page in length:

The Spirit of Agitation; Even Insight Misses the Point; What is Your Will; Meher Baba Planned Our Lives; Giving Up a Dream; No Way To Escape Truth.

But here I have to stop, with apologies to the reader if I am being tantalizing: there is a note at the front of the typed-up compilation he gave to each of us which says that "these notes are for your private use only. They are not to be lent, sold or reproduced." The only reason I even mention them is that they make good reading, with the advantage of being short and, in their typed up versions, tightly written and concise, and they show Don giving free rein to his own creative and interweaving thoughts on the theme of mysticism in everyday life. At the same time they are far from being merely cerebral. They are a work in progress showing Don grappling in a typically 'muscular' way with widely recognizable practical problems of life. As to why they must not be published or shared, my guess is that Don saw the danger of this more personal and speculative writing getting in the way of Baba's words, or at least providing a distraction from them.

I do however have another unpublished piece of Don's writing which arrived from him in the mail one day out of the blue. When he learned that Lisa and I had been to New Mexico and were fascinated by the high desert flora and fauna, Don said he too had a lasting interest in deserts, especially those of the Southwestern United States, reminding us he was a native of Nevada, a desert state. The essay he sent is from his undergraduate days at Johns Hopkins University, with the title *Deserts*, (Don E. Stevens, Senior Comprehensive, 1940). [1]

I have read this over many times and never cease to be amazed at its brilliance - a 21 year old science undergraduate set free for this assignment to display literary skills, breadth of knowledge, and a kind of jaunty anthropomorphizing playfulness of style, all reminiscent of some seasoned and fluent communicator to the public of complex scientific matters in digestible layman's terms. A feature of the paper is Don's own special interest in man's interaction with, and effect on, the desert - and that of the desert on man. Here is the opening paragraph:

> "In his strange, heedless career of self perpetuation man has insinuated himself into habitats which seem like the last remaining protests of a nature striving to rid herself of the destructive microbic forms multiplying at the expense of her carcass. Like a wasp or moth which has been ill-fated enough to fall near the ant-road, she is soon overrun by a horde of minute, scurrying forms bent on living at her expense; in a fury she shakes her body and sends waves of the tiny intense creatures to their death, but horde after horde sweeps over her until an occasional twitch of a leg is all that remains to suggest life."

This vision predates the environmental movement and the work of Rachel Carson by a good decade, and I can't help thinking it puts an interesting slant on Don's future career in the extractive industry!

There are many little snippets that would be a pleasure to quote, but space won't allow, so here are just two more passages:

> "Usually during the months of August and September the desert region of Arizona and New

Mexico is bathed by downpours of rain which have an effect upon the desert which might give rise to a legend of a Proserpine returning to her mother Ceres. What else but a goddess could transform a barren dusty plateau with inverted ice-cream cone mountains into a garden to delight the heart of a Pan. The desert seems to rouse itself from its hoary stupor, clothes itself in lush carpets of vivid green grass, yawns, and roars as magnificent lightning flashes create and destroy silhouettes of the toothed mountains. Water pours down the arroyos, the cacti forget their forbidding grimness and join in the merrymaking by putting out exotic blooms, annuals spring up in a mad riot, and for a month the desert forgets itself in sensuous hilarity and indulgence.......like an introvert on a madcap spree, in the depths of its cups it suddenly remembers its essential moody and ingrown nature; the grasses dry up and disappear, the flowers wither, the creeks stop their flow of water, and in a trice the desert has returned to its solemn, unreal quiet."

Don concludes his essay on deserts with a consideration of man himself, reflecting perhaps his truest and deepest lifelong future interest:

"What about the people who live in such weird regions? From their mother desert they absorb a simple introversion uncorrupted by the introspection of the sport of cultured society. The result is a rather ruthless, rugged individualism with the source of all value located within the individual in question. Lacking constant close association with a group of fellow men, values and ideas become personalized, ingrained, and lacking in transfer value. Of such stuff are created the mystic, the fanatic, and the lawless with whom one associates desert living".

At the risk of appearing facetious, I can't resist drawing a few parallels here with the writer himself. Firstly, no prizes are on offer for spotting which of the personas in that final sentence may be Don. And what of the personal characteristics? Introverted? Intrinsically yes, although in that case Baba in due course turned him inside out; ruthless, in the sense of his one-pointed execution of his projects in Baba's name, yes; a rugged individualist, definitely, but with the source of all value located in Baba; values and ideas personalized and ingrained (including the aforementioned notorious stubbornness), yes; lacking in transfer value - definitely not.

V.
FORGIVENESS.

"Whether men soar to outer space or dive to the bottom of the deepest ocean they will find themselves as they are, unchanged, because they will not have forgotten themselves, nor remembered to exercise the charity of forgiveness." - Meher Baba

The various demands of life in general - and sometimes the need to mull over half formed thoughts - have often forced me to put the writing of this piece on hold, sometimes for several months at a time. During one of these lulls I was at the Meher Centre in Myrtle Beach, attending a musical evening in the Reading Room of the library, when a man I had never seen before came in and sat next to me. Sticking up out of the side pocket of his coat was a book bearing a striking photo of Don on its back cover, his eyes staring urgently out at me. The man was Laurent Weichberger, a friend and associate of Don in his closing years, who had published, with notes, a verbatim recording of a 2006, 2-day meeting of one of the so-called 'Young People's Groups'. Don had met with this group periodically since about 2003, in various places in the US, up until he passed away. The book was titled "*The Doorbell of*

Forgiveness," a copy of which Laurent presented to me the next day.

Here was a book that set me off on a track of thought on a slow fuse that is still burning away without my knowing quite what, or where, the point of detonation will be - or indeed whether there will ever be one. I say this partly because Don characterizes forgiveness as something of an avataric bombshell—my word not his—for the coming age! It's not my intention to summarize or analyze too closely the content of the book, but I feel I have to say something about it for at least two reasons: firstly, because of the passion with which Don expounds his thoughts and feelings on the subject of forgiveness; secondly, because the verbatim recording brought back to me his way of talking, his semantic idiosyncrasies, his whole atmosphere.

Reading the book made me feel with a real sense of warmth that I was in his company all over again. If I say that Don tends to dominate the conversations, if anything to a greater extent even than in my own time with him, this is no longer in a spirit of criticism. Somewhere in the book he talks about the outer shell of a sanskara, that which presents itself to the world at large in the form of a character trait, being the last thing to go after the motivating force, the stuff inside, has worn itself out. It occurred to me with a bit of a chuckle as I was reading, that this could be the case with Don; that his urgent, voluminous and passionate expansion on the subject at hand came from a place within him that was relatively free of ego. I wondered if this, therefore, evoked in me quite a different reaction from the one nearly 30 years ago—to say nothing of the part my own ego played, then and now. And on top of all this there is the strong sense that time is running out, that his deepest intuitions have to be put 'out there' for the next generation to make of them what they will, before it's too late - for us and for him.

The importance of forgiveness as a key concept for this avataric age had not impressed itself on Don until relatively late in his life. A respected former editor of the International Herald Tribune was giving a speech about the genocidal killings in the Balkans in the 1990s, making a link to the never-ending cycle of cruelty and revenge through the ages. Don's 'eureka moment' came when this man said that the only way out of this repetition, as far as he could see, was "just irrational, unconditional forgiveness." Don then had a dawning realization that forgiveness was a 'whole new field for civilization to tackle,' to look at the mechanics of it, to see how it works as a practice. And here I can insert a trio of relevant quotes that are also examples of the talking man that I so enjoyed in the book:

> "I don't know a stinking hades business about how to go about it, but nevertheless I've got to talk about it to groups who love Baba". And: "I don't got it (sic), I just have this keen keen feeling

the word forgiveness is a central tent pole...but I don't know that it is all of the tent poles...". And, thirdly: "...so remember...an avataric investment on a major scale in back of this...expect to see the incredible and impossible happen. But boy, its going to have to be based on a very very powerful conviction within oneself, started off by seeing what happens when you try forgiving one or two or three of your pet peeves or hatreds."

I find myself at this point needing to hold back from a full scale exposition of Don's thesis, realizing that for this it is well worth reading the book. Suffice it to say I have the impression that for Don, 'forgiveness' as a phenomenon seemed to be the missing piece which had finally fallen into place within a personal mosaic comprised also of intuition, forgetfulness (the deliberate act of putting things on the 'back burner') tenderness, oneness and love. As Baba's sister, Mani, tells us and shows us in a beautiful filmed interview, Baba used the same gesture for "I love you" as for "I forgive you". So would it not then follow that unconditional forgiveness and its practice must be the closest thing to the practice of love itself?

At first my reaction was one of skepticism. Not about the sentiment of forgiveness itself, so much as the possibility that Don might have been highlighting it as a special feature, a 'central tent pole' of Meher Baba's avataric cycle without the evidence to back it up, almost as if we might be able to call it 'the age of forgiveness' as an alternative to 'the age of intuition'. After all, was not the time of Jesus notable for *its* example of forgiveness as one of *His* central tent poles - not that it had then visibly taken hold as a shining feature of the Christian age?

Don's case was and is persuasive and attractive in several ways, not least when he says that Eruch had explained the enormous amount of time Baba spent in seclusion as a necessary part of the work of 'balancing the books', because this was not just the end of a cycle (of avataric ages) but 'the end of a cycle of cycles.' It occurred to me as I read this that a heavy dose of forgiveness would certainly be in order if the books were to be balanced in time. But, while convinced of the need for forgiveness in the world, I couldn't be sure that Don had not somehow just plucked it out of the air and given it a status as Baba's special gift, something we would be able to tap into as never before and make use of in overcoming the endless repetition of violence and revenge.

On the other hand, I remembered the lesson I had learned through painful experience, of the importance of my own forgiveness of my therapy patients' attacks on me - both physical and mental. In a highly memorable moment, one of my teachers had once characterized mental and emotional recovery in treatment as coming about through the repeated experience of being forgiven by one's therapist, on the same lines that an infant or a child is (we hope) spontaneously forgiven over and over again by its parent. All of this proved nothing, but recalling it kept me thinking, and wondering. This process of trying to keep an open mind is still in its early stages, and I await signs of detonation of the 'bombshell' with the same circumspection with which I await the 'breaking of Baba's silence'. That is, with the sense it will come, and maybe is already coming, in a much more subtle and unlooked-for way than any of us expect, or yet have the language to describe[1].

Once the process of thinking about all of this was consciously under way, I had to admit that signs of forgiveness in the world, and in people's minds, appeared to be all around. Once I was able to move beyond my skepticism and open up the subject for consideration, the signs seemed to come thick and fast, as if a paper trail were being laid for me to follow. I don't think I was specially privileged in this respect. I presume the clues to an answer are all around us once we start to focus and ask the right questions. And so this spate of, shall we call it, meaningful coincidences started with my finding a book I had been seeking on my shelves for some months. Titled *Markings*, it's a collection of the thoughts and written meditations of Dag Hammarskjold, the outstanding Swedish UN Secretary General of the 1950s and early 60s. I had wanted to compare it to Don's airplane notes, because these too were written on the hop, in airplanes and hotel rooms during incessant rounds of travel. As I opened it at random, the words "forgiveness breaks the cycle of causation" loomed out of the page.

These coincidences reached a kind of provisional climax with a film I had bought months before but never got round to watching. Rumination on the subject of man's cruelty to man, and on the subjects of revenge and forgiveness, had brought it back to mind. This was a film by the Polish director Andrzej Wajda called *Katyn*. In the early years of WW2 the entire officer corps of the Polish army, more than 20,000 men, was massacred by the Russians, who then blamed it on the Germans. The officers were led one by one to the edge of a pit and shot in the back of the head, and the last minutes of the film show three examples of this in graphic detail. The men are seen beginning to recite "Our Father which art in heaven..." only to be cut off in mid prayer. The very last frames of the film show one final example of this, a man who manages, by speaking fast, to get to the words "...forgive us our trespasses, as we forgive them..." before he is executed; and these are the last words spoken in the film. Of course no one will know what really happened or exactly what, if anything, was said by these men in 1940; but obviously the idea of forgiveness was in the mind of Andrzej Wadja in 2006. Here was a famed film director - who lost his own father in this atrocity - making a brilliant film about unforgivable acts in which he powerfully puts forward to the thousands who will have seen the film, and may see it in the future, the idea of forgiveness rather than revenge.

I took this cluster of little clues[2] as the beginning of an answer to my skepticism about what Don had been saying also, incidentally, in 2006! But that is not even the main point I want to make here, which is that on hearing the "Our Father" prayer it occurred to me that Meher Baba had given us a complete prayer about forgiveness - called *The Prayer of Repentance* - every word of which He tells us carries His own special charge.

***

The talk of 'coincidences' may be a distraction in my coming to the end of a piece that is meant to be about Don, and not about me. On the other hand I think Don would have liked the process that I have been describing. He himself, on his own say so, was in his early days a sceptic who needed 'scientific' proof of many things as he went along: witness his low opinion of the apparently "poor material" Baba drew to him at the start of his involvement with Him. To talk of process, or work in progress, is also to talk of something that was intrinsic to Don's approach to Baba in our everyday lives; the concept of practice and experimentation; the practice of happiness (as in 'Don't worry be happy'); of forgetfulness (as in his putting things on the 'back burner'); of intuition; and now forgiveness - all on a trial and error basis. Incidentally, I don't know that Don ever actually used the word 'practice' except in passing - it does have a bit of a Buddhist ring about it - but it's implied in his whole immensely practical approach to everything we are talking about. Experimentation, testing, and eventually 'truing,' especially in relation to intuitions, were much more a part of his vocabulary, and these, especially in relation to the latter, I'm sure will be written about by those who worked with Don in the final years[3].

To say that Don himself was a deeply forgiving man is perhaps stating the obvious to those who knew him well. After all, surely it was implied in his very attitude of total nonjudgmental acceptance of all the young people who came his way. That is not to say that this came easily to him: lovingkindness was a part of Don's nature that I think was drawn to the surface by Baba's loving treatment of him. But it seems to me that Don's forgiving nature might also have been a very interesting legacy of his highly disciplined Sufi background, in the sense that he was able to hold back all signs of annoyance or anger and present the face that he wanted to present, to the world at large. I don't claim that this is the same as 'forgiveness', but to me it implies that the practice of forgiveness implies a great deal of will-power, especially in the withholding of a show of anger, even to get to first base. I'm pretty sure he had been working on this long before he ever saw the attitude of forgiveness as the 'avataric bombshell' that he perceived in his closing years.

Having said all this about Don's ideas on forgiveness in general, I am also aware that buried among the motives for my writing is a nagging doubt as to whether Don ever completely forgave me for what I believed he saw as a betrayal all those years ago, and that therefore some reparation (as for instance in writing about him) may be in order. Even so, my main consciously held reason for writing comes from my sense of great luck and gratitude for having known such an extraordinary person.

In a recent book by Don and companions[4] I read that Baba had said that Don had an almost perfect balance of head and heart. I like the 'almost' in that: to my mind it's what makes him, along with his imperfections, the slightly less than perfect human being to whom at one time I was able to relate in a completely relaxed - and human - kind of way, while also being aware that he was one of my main connections to the One who was perfect, Meher Baba. Questions occasionally arise as to Don's status in Baba's wider circle, for instance as to whether he was equal to the Mandali, if not one himself. Besides not knowing the answer to that, I have never had much interest in the question. As I see it, his 'imperfections' - his perceived rigidity, lapses in judgement, his sensitivity to criticism, his 'right wing politics', his occasional indiscretions, and no doubt much else besides - can be put alongside his many gifts, which anyway far outweighed the defects. Together they combined to form a texture that made Don the man that Baba used to tremendous effect out in the world, as a man of the world.

This, then, was the man who opened to me and many others, the door to the 'ball game of life' - a blend of practical know-how in a spiritual approach to daily affairs, coupled with a willingness to take a calculated risk, informed by the wisdom of Baba's guiding hand. And with all his worldliness, his 'scientific' practicality, his stubbornness, his admirable though occasionally infuriating one-pointedness, this was the most loving and humane of men who put his gifts and his defects one hundred percent at Baba's disposal, most memorably in his role as 'Baba's Man in Europe'.

A Memoir of Don Stevens
NOTES
PREFACE:

[1] 'God become man' - see *Much Silence* p24 by Tom and Dorothy Hopkinson, Gollancz, London 1974. Also, *The Godman* by Charles Purdom, chapter 7 in Allen and Unwin 1964 edition. 'Avatara' is a sanskrit word meaning 'descent'.

[2] Darshan. See note[1] in the section below titled 'London'.

[3] 'mast' - pronounced 'must'. In *Much Silence*, Tom and Dorothy Hopkinson suggest that the word may come from a Persian word meaning 'overcome'.

The definitive book on Baba's work with masts is *The Wayfarers, Meher Baba with the God-intoxicated* by William Donkin, one of Baba's mandali. Donkin simply states that 'mast' means one who is intoxicated with divine love.

NOTES
INTRODUCTION:

[1] For a lively, entertaining and moving account of Don's first meeting with Baba, see chapter 4 in Don's book *Meher Baba The Awakener of the Age*, Companion Books 1999.

[2] *Three Incredible Weeks with Meher Baba*, Sept 11 - 30, 1954' by Malcolm Schloss and Charles Purdom.

A Memoir of Don Stevens

NOTES
LONDON:

[1] Darshan in Poona. This had been scheduled before Baba's passing, to take place, as all believed, in Baba's physical presence. The setting was Guruprasad, the residence in Poona made available to Baba every summer by its owner, the Maharani of Baroda. To have a Master's darshan is to be in his sight and presence, and is essentially a gift from the Master. Baba dropped His body a few months before the 1969 Darshan, but had said that he would be giving darshan "lying down." In His Tomb, that is, but there in Poona with the full force of His physical presence.

The expression 'dropped His body' relates to the fact that a Perfect Master's 'death' is entirely within His own control, allowing Him to dispense with His body whenever and however He chooses.

[2] Delia de Leon. An early Western devotee of Baba who met Him in 1931 in England and subsequently spent much time with Him both in Europe and in India. She was very central to all of Baba's future plans for an English group. She passed away in 1993.

[3] 'Friend'. Sufis (see also note 6 below) refer to God as 'The Friend'. 'Friendship' in Sufi teaching -

as also for the Quakers - has a more general connotation of loving reciprocity which promotes the sense of oneness.

[4] The *Discourses* and *God Speaks* are arguably the two main books dictated by Baba and edited and produced under His close supervision. Joint editors of the original English (Sufism Reoriented) editions of both books were Ivy Duce and Don Stevens.

[5]] Entombment film. This was the film made of the laying down of Baba's body in the tomb at Meherabad that he had had built many years beforehand, and which was to be the main place of pilgrimage for His lovers and seekers in the coming age.

'Amartithi', the name given by Baba to denote the day of His dropping His body, and its subsequent anniversaries, means 'deathless day' in Hindi.

[6] Sufism. A form of mysticism emanating from the Middle East, predating Islam, though revitalized by Mohammed, and in the 20th century 'reoriented' by Meher Baba.

[7] Dr Ghani. A childhood friend of Baba and an early member of the Mandali, Baba's closest circle of disciples.

[8] *(the person) is ... no longer interested in the well-being of the limited self but is only interested in the Master as representing universal and undivided life. He offers all his experiences and desires to the Master, reserving neither the good nor the evil for the limited "I", stripping the ego of all content.*
Discourses p. 177. The Nature of the Ego and Its Termination. Sheriar Foundation 2000.

[9] Regarding groups and their leaders in the Baba world, see the chapter titled 'On "Elder Brothers" and Their Groups' in *Following Meher Baba, a Handbook for Baba-lovers in the New Humanity*, by Rick Chapman, 2015.

[10] Meherabad. This is the place, founded and named by Baba, a few miles outside the city of Ahmadnagar in the State of Maharashtra, India, that was His Head Quarters from the 1920s onwards, and where His Tomb is situated.

Meherazad was Baba's home in the countryside several miles from Meherabad. It was His main residence, shared with most, though not all, of His mandali, from 1954 onwards.

[11] Dhuni Fire. A fire ritual in India connected with the giving up of attachments. Baba co-opted this tradition and made it his own. There is a dhuni cer-

emony for all the Baba community, including pilgrims, on the 12th of each month at Meherabad.

[12] I was recently reminded by Hasan Selisik, a Baba lover in Istanbul, that Don had asked Baba at some point if he could leave the oil industry, to which Baba had replied in the negative, saying "who do you think put you there in the first place".

There is a video that can be seen on 'Youtube' titled the *"Meher Baba Television Hour"* in which Don Stevens was interviewed in 1995 by Fred Stankus (AMBCSC Archives). Don tells his story of this moment, and of the moments leading up to it. Also in this interview, Don gave a clear explanation of his thinking, and the evolution of his thinking, on the subject of closed groups.

[13] 'psychology'. I have always understood from Don that he saw a Jungian analyst for some time in his early to mid adulthood. Just recently Craig San Roque, a member of the early London Don group (see also his foreword to this book) wrote from his home in Australia that "it is not known by many that Don in his youth had a period of counselling with two San Francisco Jungian analysts, one of whom was a friend of the family. The comments he made to Michael on child therapy were no doubt based on personal experience".

[14] From *"Attention and Interpretation"* (1970) by the psychoanalyst Wilfred Bion (1897 - 1979): "...what is required is a positive act of refraining from memory and desire. It may be wondered what state of mind is welcomed if desires and memory are not. A term that would express approximately what I need to express is 'faith' - faith that there is an ultimate reality and truth - the unknown, unknowable, 'formless infinite' ".

[15] The definition of 'In Company' as a 'Church' was the principal reason for dissolving it. The bylaws included the words' doctrine' and 'clergy'. The non-profit status of 'In Company' could not have been defended in a US court because of the near impossibility of proving it was a Church. Don's lawyer was in the Channel Isles (UK), and it is not certain that either of them were aware of US tax laws, under which the Board members would have been personally liable for taxes if challenged by the IRS.

I have recently been told by two of the members of that last 'In Company' Board meeting, that with reference to the main purpose of 'Meher Fund' - the entity that replaced 'In Company With Meher Baba' at the meeting described - history has come full circle. The main beneficiaries of donations to Meher Fund are now the hospital and dispensary at Meherabad. This was Don's idea at the outset, so that his original intent has been, and is being, honoured.

NOTES
EUROPE:

[1] Perfidious Albion. Albion is the ancient Celtic name for Great Britain. "Perfidious Albion", or rather "la perfide Angleterre," was a term coined, appropriately enough with reference to the Marseille Seminar, by a Frenchman - the writer and diarist Jacques-Benigne Bossuet (1627 - 1704). He was referring to the French perception of England's faithlessness and treachery in its dealings with France, though he also said that "the faith of the Saviour spread even there" (ie,to England!). Napoleon Bonaparte is said to have first expressed this sentiment as "perfide Albion".

NOTES
BEADS ON A STRING:

[1] Eruch. One of Baba's very close Mandali, especially in the latter years of His life. Eruch (along with Baba's sister Mani) mastered the meaning of Baba's hand gestures quicker and better than anybody else and became the main interpreter to those who came to meet with Baba.

[2] In *The Doorbell of Forgiveness*, a verbatim transcription of a weekend meeting of Don with one of his Young People's Groups in 2007 (and quoted at some length in the final section), there is a footnote in which the editor and principal transcriber, Laurent Weichberger, points out that Baba did once explain that His time spent at these sites was for a 'clearing' of the sanskaric traces left by seekers and accumulated over centuries, in order to make way for future visitors to a revitalized spiritual site.

[3] *In Search of the Miraculous* is the title of a book by PD Ouspensky, a close adherent of Gurdjieff.

Journey To The East by Herman Hesse is the story of a group of seekers who set out towards the metaphorical 'east', only to be deserted, much to everyone's disgust, by the most lowly member, the servant of the group. One by one, members of the group lose interest and drop out, eventually leaving only the narrator still embarked on the journey. The latter then sets out to find the earliest leavers in search of a clue to what went wrong. He discovers in the end that the true Master they were all in search of was the servant of the group who had been the first to leave.

(On reflection, not really the best advertisement for a Beads Tour, or perhaps a salutary warning!).

[4] Qutub Minar. A tower - in Delhi - of red sandstone and marble inscribed with verses from the Koran, built in the 13th century to proclaim the faith of Islam in Northern India. There is a striking photo of Baba in elaborate head, face, and neck scarf and tweed overcoat, with the Qutub Minar in the background. (see photo opposite page 1).

[5] Moinuddin Chishti - a realized Sufi saint. The visit to his dargah is described more fully in the text.

[6] Jain Temple at Mt Abu in Rajasthan. The Jain religion, emanating from India, has as its central tenet non-violence and respect towards all living beings. Mahatma Ghandi adopted many Jain principles in the way he conducted his own life. The Dilwara Jain Temple is famous for its interior of elaborate and beautifully carved white marble.

[7] Baba's L-shaped room. The tiny room in a corner of the courtyard of the house in Poona belonging to His family and which He frequented after being kissed on the forehead by Babajan (see note below). At floor level there is a large flat stone on which He would strike His forehead with great force, essentially in order to retain, or regain, awareness and possession of His physical mind and body.

[8] Babajan. An extremely aged woman (in Baba's time) of Muslim background who lived beneath a particular tree in Poona, and who regularly attracted Merwan (as Baba then was) on His way home from college. She was one of the 5 Perfect Masters whose task was to initiate Merwan into full awareness of His true identity as God Man and eventually as Avatar of the new age. She started this process by one day kissing Him on the forehead.

[9] Manonash cave. A cave outside the city of Hyderabad that had particular significance for Baba's work in the closing stages of His 'New Life' period (1949-1952). 'Manonash-' or 'annihilation of the mind' - refers to the point at which "the mind with its desires, cravings and longings is completely consumed by the fire of Divine Love". (Don Stevens, *Meher Baba The Awakener of the Age*, p109)

[10] Shivaji. The Hindu warrior king (1627 - 1680) who led successful military campaigns against Mus-

lim rule in the part of India now known as the state of Maharashtra. The fort in question is one of a chain of over 300 forts that were positioned along the Western Ghats. He established the Maratha Kingdom, based on religious tolerance and the rule of law. Baba said Shivaji was a minor avataric incarnation - in other words a previous (minor) incarnation of Baba Himself.

[11] Panchgani Cave. In a hilly area about 20 kms from Mahabaleshwar in Maharastra State. A cave that Baba had fortified with concrete and iron bars, used for seclusion and meditation from 1940 onwards. Also known as the Tiger Valley Cave.

[12] Kailash. One of a complex of cave temples at Ellora in the region of Poona, dating back to the 6th to the 13th centuries, showing examples of Hindu, Buddhist and Jain architecture and sculpture. Baba visited many times. Named after the sacred Mount Kailash in Tibet.

[13] Parvardigar. Meaning 'God' (literally 'sustainer') in the Persian language. Baba started His 'Master's Prayer' with the words O Parvardigar.

[14] *The Field* by Lynne McTaggart, Harper Collins 2001. In this book (p206) there is a fascinating passage - in the context of the Beads Tours - regarding an experiment carried out by a physicist who, with

scientist colleagues, attended a 2-week tour of the sacred sites of the ancient Egyptians, at which they carried out a series of informal ceremonies, such as chanting and meditation. The main objective was to see if people engaged in meditative activities at these sites - of the kind for which they had originally been built - had a measurable effect on their recording machines. The strongest effects occurred when the group was engaged in chanting at a sacred site. "Clearly, some resonance reverberated at the sites, possibly even a vortex of coherent memory".

It's tempting to speculate that this passage may have been one of the seeds - though by no means the only one - of Don's idea for the Beads Tours.

A Memoir of Don Stevens

NOTES
DON'S WRITING
AND REFLECTIONS:

[1] A little known piece of Don's history is that he attended Black Mountain College for a freshman year before moving on to Johns Hopkins University in Baltimore. This college, just down the road from Asheville, North Carolina, was famous in the 1930s, 40s, and 50s for a revolutionary approach to learning, especially in the Arts and Literature and to some degree in the Sciences. It encouraged the fullest expression of the 'free play' of the students' own inclinations, giving them carte blanche to structure their time as they pleased. The college attracted a whole collection of alumnae that were to be famous in later years, such as Buckminster Fuller, Merce Cunningham and John Cage, to name but a few. Don's attendance here is a reminder of his early musical talent, and also perhaps of a side to his nature that was attracted to the new, to the experimental, and the slightly dangerous. The fact that he left after a year may in turn say something about a preference, or a need, for structure.

NOTES
FORGIVENESS:

[1] 'silence'. In contrast to my tentative speculations regarding the breaking of His silence, consider some of Baba's own words as recorded in Francis Brabazon's *Stay With God*, (1959 Garuda Books Edition p66).

> "When I break my silence... It will reverberate in all people and creatures... The effective force of this Word in individuals and their reaction to It will be in accordance with the magnitude and receptivity of each individual mind. And the reaction will be as instantaneous and as various as the reaction of people in a room through which a cobra suddenly and swiftly passes, when some would nervously laugh, some lose control of their bowels and some feel great courage or reasonless hope and joy."

[2] Another film I saw in the described sequence of 'coincidences' was "*Philomena*", with Judy Dench as the Irish lady who had been deprived of her small son, for adoption against her will, by the nuns of the institution that had held her (one of the notorious Magdalen convents). When she returns to confront the one surly and unrepentant nun surviving from the time she was an inmate, she unexpectedly and

spontaneously forgives her. A deeply moving and powerful moment.

[3] Intuition. See *Meher Baba's Gift of Intuition 15 Essays*. By Don Stevens and Companions. Companion Books 2006.

[4] *Three Snapshots of Reality* by Don Stevens with Wayne Smith. Companion books 2014.

ACKNOWLEDGEMENTS

Many thanks to Leah Florence and Elizabeth Heaney for their expert reading of several drafts, and for their very helpful suggestions; and to Karl Moeller who carried me and the Memoir through the whole process of publishing.

Also thanks to my friends in England, Robert and Georgina Hartford, whose comments spurred me on.

And not least thanks to my wife Lisa, whose lucid opinions and support have been a bedrock before, during and since the writing of this piece.

www.ingramcontent.com/pod-product-compliance
Ingram Content Group UK Ltd.
Pitfield, Milton Keynes, MK11 3LW, UK
UKHW041227200426
11947UKWH00034B/203